SEASONS OF HUNGER

Seasons of Hunger

Fighting Cycles of Quiet Starvation Among the World's Rural Poor

Stephen Devereux, Bapu Vaitla
and Samuel Hauenstein Swan

Foreword by
Robert Chambers

PLUTO PRESS
www.plutobooks.com

in association with

First published 2008 by Pluto Press
345 Archway Road, London N6 5AA

www.plutobooks.com

British Library Cataloguing in Publication Data
A catalogue record for this book is available from the British Library

ISBN   978 0 7453 2827 0   Hardback
ISBN   978 0 7453 2826 3   Paperback

Library of Congress Cataloging in Publication Data applied for

10   9   8   7   6   5   4   3   2   1

Designed and produced for Pluto Press by
Chase Publishing Services Ltd, Sidmouth, EX10 9QG, England
Typeset by Stanford DTP Services, Northampton, England
Printed and bound in the European Union by
CPI Antony Rowe, Chippenham and Eastbourne

'The Great Tablecloth'

When they were called to the table,
the tyrants came rushing
with their temporary ladies;
it was fine to watch the women pass
like wasps with big bosoms
followed by those pale
and unfortunate public tigers.

The peasant in the field ate
his poor quota of bread,
he was alone, it was late,
he was surrounded by wheat,
but he had no more bread;
he ate it with grim teeth,
looking at it with hard eyes.

In the blue hour of eating,
the infinite hour of the roast,
the poet abandons his lyre,
takes up his knife and fork,
puts his glass on the table,
and the fishermen attend
the little sea of the soup bowl.
Burning potatoes protest
among the tongues of oil.
The lamb is gold on its coals
and the onion undresses.
It is sad to eat in dinner clothes,
like eating in a coffin,
but eating in convents
is like eating underground.

Eating alone is a disappointment,
but not eating matters more,
is hollow and green, has thorns
like a chain of fish hooks
trailing from the heart,
clawing at your insides.

Hunger feels like pincers,
like the bite of crabs,
it burns, burns and has no fire.
Hunger is a cold fire.
Let us sit down soon to eat
with all those who haven't eaten;
let us spread great tablecloths,
put salt in the lakes of the world,
set up planetary bakeries,
tables with strawberries in snow,
and a plate like the moon itself
from which we can all eat.

For now I ask no more
than the justice of eating.

                                    Pablo Neruda

Contents

List of Illustrations

FIGURES

BOXES

The Action Against Hunger / Action contre la Faim international network (ACF) helps more than 4.2 million people in 43 countries worldwide. It is comprised of Action Against Hunger-UK (ACF-UK), Action contre la Faim-France (ACF-France), Acción contra el Hambre-Spain (ACF-España), Action Against Hunger-USA (ACF-USA) and Action contre la Faim-Canada (ACF-Canada).

For over 25 years, ACF has been at the forefront of the fight against hunger and malnutrition worldwide. Its vocation is to save lives, especially those of malnourished children, and to work with vulnerable populations to preserve and restore their livelihoods with dignity. ACF's activities include the diagnosis, treatment and prevention of malnutrition, as well as food security, water and sanitation, and basic health programmes.

In 2005, ACF launched Hunger Watch, its policy research and advocacy department. Hunger Watch's concern is to identify the causes of, responsibilities for, and responses to current food crises. The Hunger Watch team examines transversal factors such as conflict, market instability, gender and HIV/AIDS, and analyses their linkages to acute hunger.

Hunger Watch also visits households affected by malnutrition to collect first-hand testimonies and engage in discussions pertaining to the experience of living with hunger. Hunger Watch additionally develops tools for comparing the extent and severity of nutritional crises across the globe. This book is part of the Hunger Watch series of publications produced by the research and advocacy team in London.

Institute of
Development Studies

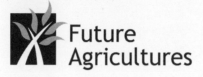

Future
Agricultures

The Institute of Development Studies (IDS) is a leading global organisation for research, teaching and communications on international development. IDS was founded in 1966 and enjoys an international reputation based on the quality of its work and its commitment to applying academic skills to real world challenges. Its purpose is to understand and explain the world, and to try to change it – to influence as well as to inform.

The Future Agricultures Consortium (www.future-agricultures.org) is a partnership involving research-based organisations in Africa (Ethiopia, Kenya and Malawi) and the United Kingdom (the Institute of Development Studies, Imperial College London, and the Overseas Development Institute), with core funding from the UK Department for International Development (DFID). The Consortium aims to encourage critical debate and policy dialogue on the challenges of establishing and sustaining pro-poor agricultural growth in Africa, through stakeholder-led policy dialogues on future scenarios for agriculture, informed by in-depth field research.

Foreword

Of all the dimensions of rural deprivation the most neglected is seasonality. Vulnerability, sickness, powerlessness, exploitation, material poverty, under- and malnutrition, wages, prices, incomes … these are recognised, researched and written about. But among them again and again seasonality is overlooked and left out.

Yet seasonality manifests in all these other dimensions and in how they interlock. This is almost universal for poor people, but especially so in the rural tropics. There, during the rains, poor people are repeatedly oppressed and screwed down by a cruel combination of lack of food, lack of money, high food prices, physical hardship, hard work vital for survival, debilitating sicknesses such as diarrhoeas and malaria, and isolation and lack of access to services. It is then that they are materially most poor, most vulnerable, most powerless, most exploited, most isolated, and most short of food. It is then that these dimensions most tightly interlock and reinforce each other. It is then that poor people suffer most and are most vulnerable to becoming poorer.

It is also when they are most invisible. Integrated seasonal poverty is matched and mirrored by integrated professional ignorance. Professionals anyway focus on their own specialised disciplinary concerns and miss linkages with those of others. This is compounded when all professions overlook seasonality. They do not see the stark and cyclical reality of the seasons when deprivations collide and hit poor people simultaneously. So research, reports and recommendations repeatedly omit the seasonal dimension. Papers published on rural poverty in the tropics often never mention it. I have never once read or heard it in the speech of a policy-maker. It is simply missing from most professionals' and policy-makers' mental maps.

The reasons are not far to seek. We development professionals are season-proofed – insulated and protected by our housing, air conditioning, fans and heaters, clothing, urban facilities, incomes, food supplies, protection from infection, and access to health services. Often we gain impressions most from rural elites, but as this book points out, while seasonality is bad for the poor it can be good for the rich. We are also season-blind – we travel least at the bad times during the rains and before the harvest, and when we do, stick more than ever to tarmac and places close to town. Except in full-blown famines, we rarely encounter or perceive the regular seasonal hardship, hunger and starvation of remoter poor people. Cyclical seasonal hunger is quiet and hidden. When the rains are over, the harvest is in, and people are through the worst, urban-based professionals travel again and venture further afield. Their impressions are then formed at the best times, missing the worst.

This book is a powerful corrective. It brings a new perspective and proposals for action that are new in their scope and focus. It shows how central seasonality is to the creation and deepening of deprivation. The case is made, irrefutably, that seasonal hunger is the father of famine and that famine cannot be stopped unless seasonal hunger is stopped.

What is so shocking is the evidence of how policies have made it worse. In earlier decades, in many countries, with parastatal marketing boards, people in remote areas were entitled and able to buy seed and sell crops at fixed prices which did not vary by season. With enforced liberalisation and the abolition of the boards, the poor people in those areas, and elsewhere, lost that protection and were once again exposed to cruel seasonal fluctuations in prices. The market did not serve them. It exposed them. Liberalisation made poor people poorer, and created conditions for famines in bad years.

The situation cries out for action. Drawing on their experience and research, Devereux, Vaitla and Hauenstein Swan show what has to be done. They bring together proposals for a raft of workable measures for social protection. Agricultural livelihood development is basic. Emergency and social protection measures include: nutritional and food security surveillance; community-based management of acute malnutrition; cash and food transfers; seasonal employment programmes; social pensions; child growth promotion; and crop insurance schemes. And these are costed. The question becomes not whether they can be afforded but whether governments, lenders and donors who are serious about poverty can conceivably not afford them.

To end seasonal hunger, rights and power are crucial. This is shown by India's employment guarantee schemes. Poor people must have rights to make demands. There must be an enforceable right to food. The persuasive argument put forward is for a 'fundamental transformation in the political obligations around hunger'.

This book is a wake up call. After *Seasons of Hunger*, things should never be the same again. It should be required reading for all development professionals – political leaders, officials, those who work in governments, aid agencies and NGOs, academics, researchers, teachers, local leaders and others – all who are committed to the fight against poverty. For all those who share that commitment, it is a 'must'. Let us in the future always find 'seasonality' in books, articles and reports on poverty. In committees, meetings and reviews of policy and practice, and in research, let there always be someone who asks and presses the question: 'And what about seasonality?' Let that crucial, pervasive, cross-cutting dimension never again be overlooked or ignored. To achieve that, we have to start with ourselves, our own perceptions and priorities. To make poverty history, we have to make seasonal blindness history.

The development community has a huge, historic opportunity. It is precisely because seasonal deprivation has been so neglected that it now presents such immense and wide-ranging scope for attacking poverty. Any development professional serious about poverty has now, more than ever, to be serious about seasonality. May the right to food be recognised. May the measures advocated here be adopted. And so let us banish the hidden obscenity of quiet seasonal starvation from our world and make seasonal hunger history.

Seasons of Hunger shows how.

Robert Chambers
29 May 2008

Preface

The headlines are distressing. Over the past several years, and particularly in recent months, food prices across the world have skyrocketed. Governments from Haiti to Senegal to Indonesia face populaces seething with anger. Expressions of protest, through ballot boxes as well as street riots, threaten and in some cases have already toppled ruling parties. Millions of children find themselves at elevated risk of malnutrition. The prospect of the situation improving in the near future is bleak.

With the worsening of this 'world food crisis', the issue of hunger is back at the forefront of the global political agenda, and deservedly so. The deeper truth, however, is that for hundreds of millions of people in the world, extreme hunger and malnutrition were a 'normal' part of life long before the current crisis made the front page. Journalists and activists will, justifiably, highlight today's particular circumstances – 'the perfect storm' of higher oil and fertiliser prices, increasing global demand for grain, diversion of croplands to biofuel production, the impact of climate change on food production, and so on[1] – but the root causes of the present situation are the same as those that have driven hunger for generations: poverty, price volatility, and low agricultural productivity. Policy responses to the current crisis must thus be careful not to miss the forest for the trees. Biofuel production should indeed be questioned, food import and export rules should be recalibrated, and so on; but the more fundamental issues should not, once again, be left unaddressed – most importantly, that the poor require cash to be able to pull the free market and its food towards them, that protection against price shocks is an indispensable part of fighting hunger, and that growth in agricultural production cannot be taken for granted.

This book is not primarily about today's world food crisis. It is rather about the permanent world food crisis: seasonal hunger among the rural poor, the cycles of quiet, predictable starvation that injure and kill tens of millions of people every year.

Nearly seven out of every ten hungry people in the world, or about 600 million, are either part of small farm households or are landless rural workers.[2] Many of these 600 million live in areas where water or temperature constraints allow only one crop harvest per year. Their poverty is driven by seasonal cycles, worsening especially in the pre-harvest months.[3] During this 'hunger season' period, the food stocks left over from the last harvest are running low and a similar general shortage in the local economy pushes food prices to unaffordable levels. To make matters worse, the hunger season is often also the peak disease season: the pre-harvest months are usually the rainy months, when malaria, diarrhoeal diseases and other illnesses strike hardest. Sick people lose their appetites, have trouble absorbing nutrients, and struggle to retain what they have eaten. All of these difficulties collide to create seasonal patterns of hunger and malnutrition, especially among the smallest children.

This suffering is not inevitable. The challenges in fighting seasonal hunger are formidable, but can be overcome with the right mix of ideas, enough money to back the implementation of these ideas, and the laws to guarantee that implementation is honest and committed. This last point is central: thus far the struggle against hunger has rested on the inconstant foundation of charity pleas and political will, and the results have been predictably fragile and limited. Only when access to food becomes a question of human rights and justice is the end of hunger realistically achievable.

At the present moment, the realisation of this 'justice of eating' seems distant; but the stakes – the health and lives of the world's people, and most distressingly the world's children – are too high to balk at distance and difficulty. It is up to all of us together, the citizens of the world, to assert to our leaders that ending hunger is in fact our greatest political interest. At the very least, we must try our very best.

Community members of Geni village, Malawi, discuss their seasonal calendar in a participatory exercise conducted for this book.

Acknowledgements

This book is based mainly on field research conducted by the authors in various countries, primarily Malawi and India, but also Niger, Ethiopia, Ghana and Namibia. In each of these locations, our work would not have been possible without the assistance of a great number of people, including members of the communities we visited, Action Against Hunger staff, and personnel of government agencies and non-governmental organisations.

In Malawi, we would like to thank the Action Against Hunger team, including Hervé Cheuzeville, Elena Rivero, Raquel Argibay, David Chibaka, Smart Massamba, Stella Sibande, Isaac Kalilombe, Madalitso Banda, Maxwell Khombe, Frank Jantala, Madalo Bvumbwe, Chimemwe Jere and Nynke Nutma. We are grateful to the people of Geni and Kasiya, particularly Devison Banda and his family, Faliot Chiputu, Grace Chisale, Mirion Nkhoma, Gladys Taurino, Agnes Andeson, Esther Chilangiza, Charity Banda, the members of Umodze and the staff of St Andrews Hospital. We would also like to thank the officials of the Malawian government, including Dr Mary Shewa, Principal Secretary of the Department of Nutrition and HIV/AIDS, Tapiwa Ngulube and Felix Pensulo Phiri of the Ministry of Health, and the many district officers in the vicinity of Geni and Kasiya who assisted us. We would also like to thank various civil society and donor agency officials in Lilongwe, including representatives of CONCERN, MALEZA, the European Commission, Irish Aid and USAID, for their opinions and insights.

The work in Niger would not have been possible without the help of the ACF missions in Niamey and Bamako. We would like to express our gratitude to Sébastien Bouillon, Michael Flachaire, Dera Salifou Mahamadou, Elisa Dominguez Muriel and Maria Segovia in Niamey, Mariama Ousmane for her excellent work as our field research assistant, the entire project team in Keita, including Laurent Teuličres, Marie Doutremepuich, Fati Amadou, Romain Florent and Wakengue Wakilongo, for their flexibility, local guidance and the detailed knowledge they passed on to us. We would like to acknowledge the European Commission, CONCERN and UMEC for taking the time to meet with us.

In India, we would like to thank Lakshmi Vaitla and Pattabhi Vaitla for their considerable support, as well as Satya Sree Kothapalli and the entire Kothapalli family, Balamurali Krishna Prasad Kondepati, Sirisha Kondepati and the entire Kondepati family, Ganesh Dhokane, Hari Krishna Taneer, Sai Harini and Manna Vishnu Murthy for their help in the field. A special thanks to Spurthi Reddy and Navjyoti from the Right to Food Campaign for interviews – and, more importantly, for their tremendous work. We also would like to thank the many officials of the Indian government in West Godavari and Mahabubnagar districts who assisted us, particularly from the Department of Rural Development, the Department of Women and Child Development and the Department of Agriculture. We would also like to thank the people of Annapanenivari Gudem and Jaklair for giving of their time so generously, including the staff of the Anganwadi centres, particularly Kumari and Saromani from Annapanenivari Gudem.

We would like to thank Angelina Lawrence, Jean-Michel Grand, Henri Leturque, Christine Kahmann, Jamie Anderson, Steve and Sarah Fonte and Tree Kilpatrick for their valuable feedback and assistance in editing. We are indebted to numerous individuals in the technical and operational teams of ACF, who have given the resources and assistance for us to conduct this work. A special thanks to Alison Hauenstein Swan for enduring this winter of research and writing, and for her support all the way through.

Financial support towards the cost of this publication was provided by the Institute of Development Studies and the Future Agricultures Consortium.

Finally, and most importantly, we would like to thank the men, women and children in every community we visited for volunteering their time and their stories, as well as the leaders and elders for being such excellent hosts. This book is dedicated to them, in the hope that it proves to be of some benefit in easing the pain of hunger all over the world.

List of Abbreviations

ADMARC	Agricultural Development and Marketing Corporation (Malawi)
BMI	Body Mass Index
CBM	Community-Based Management (of acute malnutrition)
CESCR	Committee on Economic, Social and Cultural Rights
CFA	Communaute Financière Africaine (Nigerian currency)
CRC	Convention on the Rights of the Child
DECT	Dowa Emergency Cash Transfers project (Malawi)
FACT	Food and Cash Transfers project (Malawi)
FSI	Food Stress Index
GDP	Gross Domestic Product
GNP	Gross National Product
ICC	International Criminal Court
ICDS	Integrated Child Development Services (India)
ICESCR	International Covenant on Economic, Social and Cultural Rights
ICJ	International Court of Justice
IFAD	International Fund for Agricultural Development
MK	Malawian Kwacha (currency)
NFRA	National Food Reserve Agency (Malawi)
NGO	Non-Governmental Organisation

NREGA	National Rural Employment Guarantee Act (India)
NREGS	National Rural Employment Guarantee Scheme (India)
NRU	Nutritional Rehabilitation Unit
PDS	Public Distribution System (India)
PSNP	Productive Safety Nets Programme (Ethiopia)
PUCL	People's Union for Civil Liberties (India)
RTFC	Right to Food Campaign
RUF	Ready-to-Use Food
TFC	Therapeutic Feeding Centre
USAID	United States Agency for International Development

1
Those with Cold Hands

The poor? They are those who have cold hands …
(from discussion with community members
in Geni village, Mchinji district, Malawi)

Devison Banda walks slowly up the red clay path, hoe hanging loosely from his fingers, sweat dripping down his face. He does not look surprised to see us, three researchers from the city with note pads and pencils in hand, sitting on a log near his house; perhaps a neighbour informed him of our arrival. He smiles greetings as we rise to shake hands.

It is a hot afternoon in the village of Kasiya in central Malawi, the fifth consecutive clear day in the midst of the rainy season – beautiful weather if you are a field researcher, dangerous weather if you are a farmer. Another week without rain and the fields of maize around us will begin to wilt. Devison suggests that his uncle's shed, a small, sturdy structure of brick and mortar, would be a comfortable place to sit and talk. His uncle is the village headman, and one of the few people in the community who could afford to build such a shed. Most of the surrounding houses, including Devison's own, are built of wood and thatch.

Figure 1.1   Devison Banda in his uncle's shed in Kasiya village, Malawi.

Copyright © Bapu Vaitla.

We chat with Devison at length, trying to learn more about the lives of the people in the village. He tells us that this past year was not catastrophic, certainly not like the terrible year of 2002, when nine people in Kasiya died

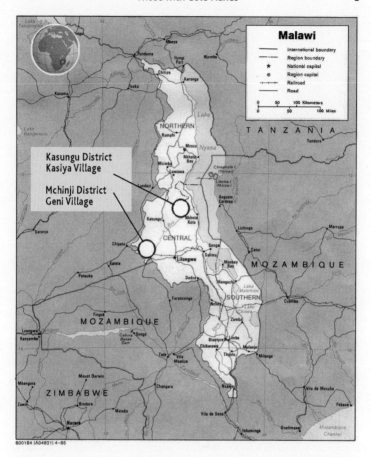

Figure 1.2   Kasiya and Geni villages in Kasungu and Mchinji districts, Malawi.

Source: www.ccafrica.ca

of hunger. But the food supplies from last year's harvest are dwindling, and the upcoming harvest is not looking promising. 'I didn't have enough money to buy fertiliser for my maize field this year,' Devison says, 'so it won't yield much.' He looks out of the shed's doorway at the clear sky and shakes his head. 'And the rain ... it's hard to say what will happen.'

We ask Devison to tell us about his daily routine at this time of the growing season, in mid-February with the harvest still two months away. 'My wife and I wake up at about five o'clock in the morning,' he begins, 'and head out right away to the fields, before it gets too hot. We try to do most of the farm work – which this time of year is mostly weeding and banking soil around the bases of the plants – before one o'clock in the afternoon, when it's time to eat the first meal.'

The three of us researchers look at each other, and then at our watches. Almost two o'clock; our conversation has delayed his first meal even longer. 'So,' our colleague Smart Massamba says to Devison, 'you haven't eaten yet today.' Devison shakes his head. 'These days, we have only two meals a day – no breakfast. It's the hunger season.'

And the two meals are, in both quality and quantity, far from what the word 'meal' might suggest. The largest meal is dinner, when the family eats *nsima*, a starchy maize product that tastes somewhat like a thick porridge. Boiled pumpkin leaves and whatever few vegetables are available are used to make a sauce; meat is almost never eaten during the hunger months. Lunch is maize porridge, essentially a thinner version of *nsima*. Between December and March, this is the daily menu for Devison's family.

Fundamentally, the causes of this seasonal hunger have to do with rainfall and poverty. In most parts of Malawi, the rainfall pattern permits only one major harvest a year, in April. Some of the better-off households in Kasiya have access to irrigated garden plots on the river banks that can be harvested several times a year. But for poorer families like Devison's there is only the single season of rainfall, and thus only a single harvest, which is rarely sufficient to feed the family all year round. The months leading up to this harvest, beginning with December, are months of hunger.

Some years are worse than others. The 2002 famine was the worst hunger in several generations, and the 2005/06 lean season was also very bad. It was in this latter period that Devison's son Krispin had to be taken to the Nutritional Rehabilitation Unit (NRU) of the local hospital, 20 kilometres away. 'He was a year old at the time. His whole body was swollen and we didn't know why,' Devison remembers. 'None of us were eating much. We had very little food while we waited for the harvest to come. The three older girls had lost a lot of weight and were very skinny, but he was the only one swollen like this. We were worried, so we took him to the hospital.' As the nurses at the NRU explained to Devison and his wife, the swelling was due to a condition called kwashiorkor, a dangerous form of malnutrition that mainly affects very young children. The exact causes of kwashiorkor are still debated, but likely have to do with a combination of micronutrient deficiency, protein deficiency, and infection. Kwashiorkor usually indicates that children are not only eating less food, but are also eating a less diverse diet; Krispin had little to eat in 2005 other than breast milk and *nsima*. If left untreated, kwashiorkor can, and often does, kill. Luckily, Krispin was taken to the NRU in time. The nurses treated him with nutrient-rich therapeutic foods, and he recovered.

But in some ways the hunger of 2005/06 never ended. Devison tells us that the search for food and medicine that year drained the family's finances. Surviving the hunger season – much less trying to rebuild their assets – became more and more difficult in subsequent years. Now they own little else but one acre of maize, far less than what is needed to feed the whole family. They try to find whatever additional work they can on other farmers' lands, but jobs are scarce in the hungry season; many other families are looking for work as well.

Devison tells us all of this in quiet, weary tones, which we at first attributed to exhaustion after a hard morning's work in the fields. Devison Banda, though, is more than tired. Like the rest of his family, he is also hungry – tired and hungry and in the middle of the same hard fight that begins every year just before Christmas.

HUNGER IN THE FIELDS

It is a bitter irony that half of the world's hungry people are farmers. But the statistic seems less strange when one considers that for many poor families, farming is an exercise in too little land, erratic rains, and soils worn out by decades of being squeezed for food. A lack of water, nutrients and good seed leads to crop yields far below biological potential, as becomes clear when we compare staple crop productivity per hectare in some of the countries mentioned in this book with productivity in the United States (Figure 1.3). In all cases, yield could at least be doubled; in Malawi, maize yields per hectare could potentially increase tenfold.

Low crop yields compel poor farming families to make decisions that provide short-term returns but have negative longer-term consequences. One example is the practice of harvesting crops in their 'green' immature stage; after the previous year's food stocks run out, there is little choice but to consume this year's harvest as soon as possible. This is an especially common practice for poor maize growers like Devison Banda. Although the caloric value of the maize

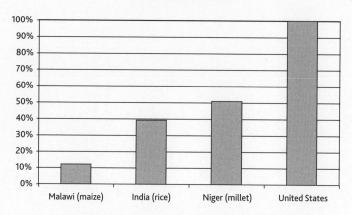

Figure 1.3 Average yield of staple crops in Malawi, India and Niger, as percentage of US average yield for each of these crops.

Source: FAO (2008a).

crop would increase greatly if the cobs were allowed to dry and then ground into flour, hunger pushes many families to harvest the immature cobs, which are then boiled and eaten immediately.

Deforesting hillsides to expand croplands is another example of sacrificing future potential for present need. Although farmers know that cultivating steep slopes will lead to erosion and eventually poor yields, in the short term the extra land may be the difference between hunger and food sufficiency. In the village of Kasiya, the hilly forest areas are thankfully still intact, and shared by the community as an important source of firewood, building materials and medicines. They are also extraordinarily beautiful: diverse multi-layered assemblages of grasses, ferns, shrubs and large hardwood trees, filled with birds and small wildlife. On the day we visited the forest, our 'guide' from Kasiya, a quiet man named Mirion Nkhoma, told us that although the community is fighting to keep the area wild, the pressures of increasing population and poverty endanger the forest's existence more and more with each passing year.

Figure 1.4   Mirion Nkhoma, in the communally-managed forest of Kasiya, Malawi.

Despite all of these challenges, some farmers do manage in good years to reap a harvest that would be large enough to feed their family the whole year round – if they had a place to store the food and keep it safe from spoilage and pests. In Northern countries, surrounded by refrigerators and grain silos and pest control companies, food spoilage is an afterthought, something that only occurs to families when the milk in the fridge has gone bad. For rural households in poor countries, the issue is much more critical: unable to afford pest-proof storage facilities and living without electrification, families must either eat or sell the harvest quickly, or risk losing a significant portion. The extent of this 'post-harvest loss' is debated within development circles, but traditionally the assumption has been that around one-quarter of all agricultural production in poor countries is lost to pests and spoilage.[1] Such a loss could amount to up to three months' worth of food.

Figure 1.5   Grain storage facilities in Guidan Koura, Niger.

Copyright © S. Hauenstein Swan.

The inability to store food also affects the production decisions a farming family makes; for example, they may choose to grow crops that are low yielding, but store better than more productive crops. The popularity of root crops throughout Sub-Saharan Africa, despite their relatively low cash value, is partially explained by the fact that farm families can store the tubers in the ground itself with minimal loss to pests. But making such a decision means that the full productive potential of the family's resources – land, labour, water, and so on – may not be fully realised.

PRICES AND THE SEASONS

Growing food, however, is not the only way to obtain it: one may buy food as well. Indeed, contrary to the popular perception that many rural households in Africa and Asia produce all their own food needs – the image of the self-sufficient farm family – most actually depend heavily on the market for their food supply. Even families with high levels of agricultural production often sell a major portion of their crop and use the income to diversify their diet, purchasing more calories and nutrients than they would have obtained from eating only the food they grew themselves. Faced with storage problems, poor families would ideally do the same: sell part of the harvest quickly to convert food into cash, which they could then save to buy food later in the year.

Several factors make this strategy difficult, however. One is that prices for food in the post-harvest time are usually very low, due to the fact that the market is flooded by many other farmers also trying to sell their newly harvested crop. Conversely, prices for food are usually very high in the hunger season because few farmers have crops to sell at this time. Figure 1.6 illustrates this phenomenon for millet (the chief staple food) in northern Ghana, and for maize in Mchinji district, Malawi. The price of millet in northern Ghana increased by about 50 per cent between harvest time and the peak of the hunger season in 1988/89. This same pattern was repeated with maize in Malawi in 2000/01 (the year before the famine), but to a much greater extent: maize prices spiralled up by more than 400 per cent between harvest and hunger season, before falling back again at harvest time. The scale and unpredictability of these seasonal price fluctuations are responsible for much of the seasonal hunger that occurs every year in many poor countries across the world.

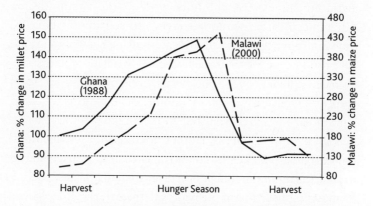

Figure 1.6   Price fluctuations of millet in northern Ghana 1988/89 and maize in Mchinji district in Malawi in 2000/01.

Sources: Devereux (1992) for Ghana data, Government of Malawi (2001) for Malawi data.

Seasonal price fluctuation is an odd phenomenon for Northern consumers to consider: imagine that all the prices in the local supermarket doubled or trebled for three months of the year. Why does such volatility happen in poor countries? There are several reasons. One is that storage in pest-proof facilities is expensive, and grain traders pass on these costs to consumers. Furthermore, since only a few wealthy traders can afford the costs, a lack of competition can drive prices even higher. In addition, the fact that many rural communities are often poorly integrated into larger national and global economies, mainly due to weak transport connections to cities and ports, also contributes to seasonal price fluctuations. Although in any given season grain supplies usually exist *somewhere* nearby, either in the same country or in neighbouring countries, the poor marketing infrastructure makes the costs of moving food from one market to another very high for traders, and once again consumers feel the impact. Thus farm families are caught in a 'price scissors', having to sell low at harvest time and buy (the same food!) high during the lean season. The food value of their cash declines considerably as the months go by.

Another reason why poor families struggle to save their harvest earnings is that, just as food storage facilities do not exist in many rural areas, neither do 'cash storage' facilities such as banks. Overall, less than 10 per cent of people living in rural areas of poor countries access formal financial services.[2] Without financial service providers to store their money safely – and to pay some interest on their savings – cash becomes a risky asset to hold.

Finally, many farm families find it difficult to save a large portion of their harvest profits because they have incurred serious debts over the growing season. Poor families borrow heavily over the course of a normal year to buy agricultural inputs, medicines and emergency food supplies during the hunger season. Lacking access to formal financial institutions, families regularly pay annual interest rates of 100 per cent or more to borrow money from local moneylenders.[3] This debt usually comes due at the harvest time, and there is often little left to be saved for the rest of the year. The lack of access to financial services tailored to their needs is thus crippling for the poor. Effective financial services could not only help buy food in the hunger season and store cash safely, but could also allow improvements in livelihood productivity – for example through the purchase of agricultural inputs like fertiliser or oxen for ploughing – and longer-term investments in health and education.

Thus high food prices, and especially seasonal price spikes, play an important role in causing hunger. But it is also important to remember that food price increases can affect people in the same community differently. The poorest households are often those with little land and a smaller harvest to meet their own food consumption needs. They depend heavily on the market for food, and are thus affected more strongly by prices than farmers with larger tracts of land (and better access to inputs like fertiliser and water), who may be able to fulfil all or almost all of their family's food needs solely from their own production. If these larger farmers have a surplus to sell, they may even benefit from the high hunger season prices. One study, for example, found that a 10 per cent increase in the price of maize in Malawi would have a negative impact on the income of households overall, with the poorest households affected the most. 'Less poor' and 'average' households are less affected than the poorest by the high prices because they depend less on the market, and the richest 20 per cent actually gain from higher prices by selling their surplus crop (Figure 1.7).

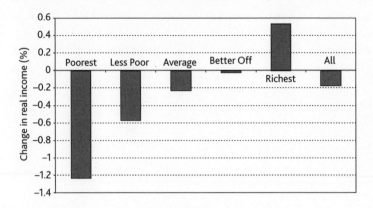

Figure 1.7   Projected effect of a 10 per cent increase in maize prices on welfare of different wealth groups in rural Malawi.

Source: FAO (2008b).

THE STRUGGLE TO FIND WORK

For many small farmers, the food and cash gained from agriculture is simply not enough to feed their families year-round. Along with the millions of poor rural families worldwide who have no land at all, they must search for additional work throughout the year. In many rural areas of poor countries, however, regular employment is impossible to find and families often scrape by day-to-day, perhaps working on a wealthier neighbour's farm one day, selling firewood the next. In very difficult times, family members, or even entire families, may migrate long distances in search of employment.

The story of Zara, a woman farmer from Guidan Koura, a village in Niger, typifies this struggle to find work. Like many of Niger's communities, Guidan Koura is located in a harsh

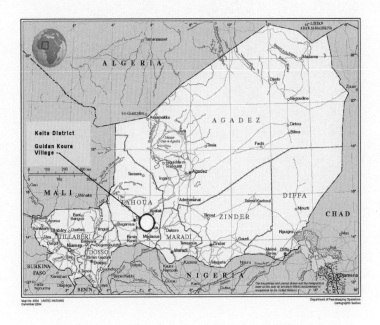

Figure 1.8   Guidan Koura village in Keita District, Niger.

Source: ReliefWeb.

semi-desert environment; rain falls only a few months of the year, and irrigation sources are few. Hunger returns every year between April and harvest time in September.

'My farm is small,' Zara tells us, 'more like a garden. And the soil is poor. It gives us no more than two months' worth of millet – in a good year – for my family. We are farmers, yes, but what we can grow is not enough.' So Zara looks for additional work to earn the money her family needs to be able to eat for the rest of the year. Like many women in Guidan Koura, she collects firewood and cattle fodder in the lands around the village, to sell at the local market or

Figure 1.9   Zara with her children, in Guidan Koura, Niger.

exchange for food. She normally earns about CFA750 (91p) daily selling what she has gathered. 'At harvest time, this is enough to buy two kilograms of millet,' she says, 'but before the harvest, prices are high and I can only buy one kilogram. Then everyone in the family needs to cut back and make do with half a portion.' In addition to gathering firewood and cattle fodder, Zara tries to find whatever other work or food she can. 'Sometimes my neighbour asks me to pound millet or sorghum for her. People try to help me, but food is scarce for everyone. Not many can afford to give us any part of the little they themselves have.'

Finding work is also difficult for Zara's husband, a traditional healer. He migrates every year to the neighbouring countries of Burkina Faso and Nigeria to search for work. 'Now and then he sends money, sometimes as much as

CFA10,000 (£12) if business is good, but I can't count on it,' Zara says. 'And sometimes he makes no money at all, and has to stay away for a year or more – like this year. I have not heard from him for months. And this also makes the planting and growing season very hard. I only have my own hands to work for my family.' During the labour migration period, called 'the time of exodus' by the community, Guidan Koura becomes a village of almost exclusively women, children and the elderly. When asked in a group discussion how they define wealth, the women of the village respond, 'To be rich is to have enough money to keep our families together throughout the year.'

Overall, Zara's family and the other poor households of Guidan Koura engage in a variety of work activities throughout the year, as Figure 1.10 shows.

And yet, despite all this varied work, hunger persists. During the lean season, Zara's family manages to eat only twice a day, and these are thin meals of porridge: millet boiled with some water and goat milk. Sometimes, when she works for her neighbours pounding millet or sorghum, she is allowed to keep the husks, which she boils and adds to the porridge; the husks make the porridge bitter, but they change the flavour of the everyday meal and make it a bit more tolerable. Overall, the lack of both food quantity and quality is a serious problem. One countrywide survey in Niger, conducted during the lean season, found that only a small percentage of children between the ages of 6 and 24 months eat fruits, vegetables, pulses and meats (Figure 1.11).

This year has been difficult for Zara and the people of Guidan Koura, but others have been worse. During the great crisis year of 2005, tens of thousands of people across Niger

Work Available	Winter			Hot Season			Rainy Season				Harvest	
	Dec	Jan	Feb	Mar	Apr	May	Jun	Jul	Aug	Sep	Oct	Nov
Agricultural work (own farm and others')	▓	▓			▓	▓	▓	▓	▓	▓	▓	▓
Firewood collection	▓	▓	▓	▓	▓	▓				▓	▓	▓
Fodder collection				▓	▓						▓	▓
Goat/sheep purchase, fattening, sales	▓	▓	▓	▓	▓	▓	▓	▓	▓	▓		
Minor activities (weaving mats, etc.)	▓	▓	▓	▓	▓	▓	▓	▓	▓	▓	▓	▓
Peak labour migration	▓	▓	▓				▓					
Peak hunger season period					█	█	█	█	█	█		

Figure 1.10 Families' labour activities by month, Guidan Koura, Niger. From participatory exercise conducted by the authors.

18

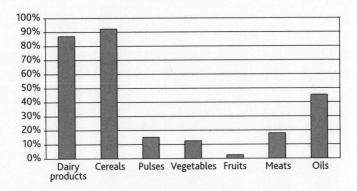

Figure 1.11 Food groups consumed by children aged 6–24 months in the 24 hours preceding survey (% of children).

Source: Government of Niger/WFP/FAO/UNICEF/FEWSNET (2008).

died in the lean season from hunger or complications resulting from hunger. Those who survived did so only through taking desperate measures. One of Zara's neighbours, Hadijata Hami, tells us that the families of Guidan Koura had to scour the bush for wild leaves to boil and eat. The social fabric of the community began to unravel; neighbours hid food from each other, knowing that dividing the food into even smaller portions would mean starvation for all. This kind of severe hunger 'turns you insane,' Hadijata says to us. 'Even if you see your father coming, you hide what food you have.' Hadijata's son eventually fell ill from malnutrition, and although he was taken to the hospital, the treatment came too late and he died. Hadijata's husband died of hunger as well a few days later, leaving her to take care of her three children alone.

Zara's story is similar. Her sister also died in the terrible year of 2005, and now Zara takes care of her sister's two children, in addition to four of her own. But with her husband having migrated in search of employment, caring for the children properly while trying to find work – and doing the taxing household chores, including walking two hours daily to fetch water – is almost impossible. 'I don't take the children with me when I go out to look for firewood. Sometimes when I'm feeling strong I'll carry one on my back,' Zara says to us. 'But usually I ask the older ones to look after the little children, to keep them asleep so they don't notice I'm gone and start to cry, and to give them some water so they don't feel as hungry.' In this lean season, her youngest child, six-month-old Jamilou, has fallen sick with malnutrition and is being treated in one of Action Against Hunger's Therapeutic Feeding Centres. Probably due to Zara's own poor nutritional status, and the little time she has for breastfeeding, her breast milk was insufficient for the small boy.

Figure 1.12   Women outside Guidan Koura returning from collecting firewood.

Copyright © S. Hauenstein Swan.

THE COSTS OF COPING

This, then, is the basic scenario of seasonal hunger for many rural people in poor countries: living in a downward spiral of low productivity and resource degradation, without adequate access to storage facilities or financial services, and in the face of escalating prices and few job opportunities, families simply run out of food and money before the next harvest comes. But the picture is incomplete without considering how the poor try to cope with these cycles, and the price of this coping.[4]

Seeking unconventional sources of income, as in the case of Zara above, is itself a type of coping strategy, and one that does not come without cost. For example, firewood harvesting – as well as the common practice of burning trees to sell charcoal – can lead to deforestation. Fodder collection from wild ecosystems, if done at high intensity, can permanently degrade the resource base. Seeking supplementary employment has direct impacts on families as well, as it generally comes at the expense of taking care of the family's own crops. A quick glance at the seasonal income source graph from Guidan Koura (Figure 1.10 above) shows that the hunger season overlaps with the time of agricultural work on families' own farms. Thus families have to choose between working to earn food for today and taking care of their own crops to grow more food for tomorrow. In Kasiya village, the poorest families' maize harvest lasts only two to three months, and as one farmer named Vayaleti Nkhoma told us, the low yields are partially due to 'late planting of land. [Many families] are too busy assisting better-off farmers because they need to work for food during the farming season. So the rich farmers' land gets first priority and the farms of the poor get last priority. By the time the rains start, poor farmers have not even prepared their land and they are too late to plant on time.' The wage rate for working on the farms of better-off families also drops precipitously in the hunger season. In Kasiya, a day's weeding early in the farming season earns MK250 (91p) or enough to buy 4 kilograms of maize, but in the hunger season, the wage rate falls by half as more families flood the labour market.

Beyond seeking alternative sources of income, the first coping strategy in response to hunger is to adjust food consumption ('rationing'), as families like Devison's and Zara's do by reducing the number of meals and the quality of the diet. In the short term, the damage from such a constriction of diet can be minimal. But continuing this practice for too long or too severely will have permanent effects, especially on the growth and development of young children. Along with food consumption, expenditure on non-food items is reduced, and often this means cutting spending on very important needs like preventative medical care or children's school fees.

Selling their possessions is another way by which poor families try to earn money during the hunger season, but the sale of productive assets like livestock, tools and land undermines the family's future ability to generate income and produce food. If this process of asset erosion continues year after year, families can find themselves in a state of extreme destitution, with a shrinking buffer against seasonal hunger. The coping strategy itself also weakens over time, for instance as the livestock herd diminishes year after year until no animals are left. In addition, because so much power is in the hands of the buyer during the hunger season, the price gained from such 'distress sales' of assets is often very low. During the 2002 famine in Malawi, livestock and household assets (radios, furniture, even kitchen utensils and clothes) were sold for less than half of their real value. One man told us of bartering his bicycle for a single bag of dried cassava; another woman spoke of exchanging clothes for a small plate of maize flour.[5]

If asset sales do not generate the income needed to buy enough food, households may also try to reduce the number of mouths that need to be fed. This can happen by an adult migrating elsewhere in search of work, such as Zara's husband does, or by sending children to relatives who might be able to better take care of them. Although the family may thus ease the economic burden, one can imagine the deep emotional cost of fathers and mothers leaving their children, and of sons and daughters being sent away.

Households may also ask relatives or friends for direct cash or food assistance – but usually very reluctantly, as it often implies a loss of dignity and self-respect. The 'social cost' of asking for such help differs from culture to culture, and so this coping strategy is exercised more easily in some places than others, but in general families will be in extreme distress before they resort to soliciting assistance.

Once all of these coping strategies have been exhausted, then truly desperate measures begin to be employed – taking loans at interest rates that will take years to pay back, begging, or even prostitution and stealing to survive. Finally, in near-famine conditions, entire families may sell their land and migrate away from home. As coping strategies become more severe and irreversible, the prospects for the family's future grow bleaker.

Figure 1.13 shows how rural families in Ethiopia, Namibia, Malawi and Ghana respond to seasonal hunger and food crises; the bars represent the percentage of households exercising each type of coping strategy. The sequence of

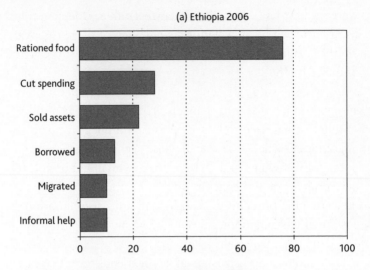

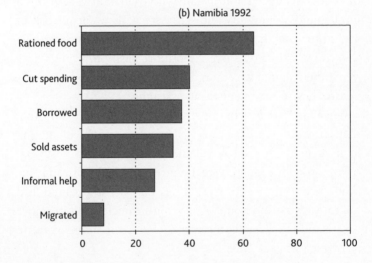

Figure 1.13   Responses to seasonal hunger in four different African countries.

Source: Devereux (2007c).

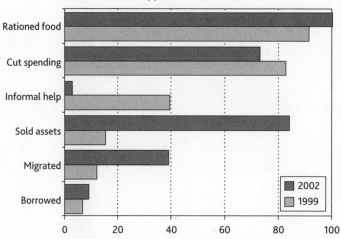

(c) Malawi 1999 & 2002

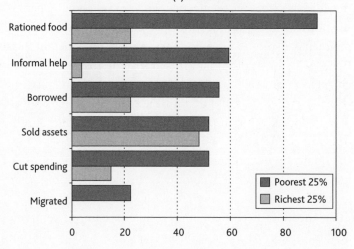

(d) Ghana 1988

coping strategies – from food rationing to cutting spending to selling assets and so on – is remarkably similar across these very different countries in different time periods.

Figure 1.13(d), taken from a minor food crisis in Ghana in 1988, is broken down by socio-economic class to illustrate how seasonality affects the rich and poor differently. As the graph shows, the poorest 25 per cent of families in affected villages were more likely to adopt all six types of coping strategies than the wealthiest 25 per cent in the same villages. Almost all poor households, but less than one in four better-off households, rationed their food consumption before the next harvest, and more than half of the poor households sought informal help, borrowed, sold assets and cut their spending. Better-off households adopted fewer strategies – none of them migrated, for instance – but the strategies they did use were more effective. For example, many better-off households sold assets to raise cash for food, but they might have sold a single cow while their poor neighbours (who owned no cattle) had to sell several goats, sheep and chickens to buy the same amount of food. So seasonality can be bad for the poor but good for the rich – it can make poor people poorer but rich people richer as they profit from the desperate efforts of the poor to survive the hunger season. If the poor are *buying* grain, *borrowing* cash, *hiring out* their labour and *selling* their land, it is the rich who are *selling* grain, *lending* cash, *hiring in* labour and *buying* land. The imbalance in power sometimes results in painfully extreme actions. In northern Ghana during the 1988 food crisis, some families 'betrothed' daughters as young as twelve to the sons of rich families for an advance bride-price payment. Being too young for marriage, these girls were destined to work in virtual slavery as house-servants for several years.

CHILD MALNUTRITION IN THE LEAN SEASON

When we first approached Devison Banda's property, we saw no one. It was several minutes before we noticed the small pair of eyes peeking out behind the doorframe of the cooking hut. Our colleague David Chibaka called out to the child in Chichewa, the local language, asking about Devison. There was no answer. David tried a few more times. Still not getting a response, he walked to the door of the hut. A little girl looked up at him with a mixture of annoyance and shyness.

'Why didn't you come out?' asked David bemusedly. 'Didn't you hear us?' Her shyness faded, leaving only the annoyance. 'I'm cooking porridge,' she said, pointing to an iron pot. 'My parents will come home for lunch any moment now.' In other words: leave me alone. When Devison speaks to us later of his children, he cannot help but smile and shake his head when he speaks of Livnes, the nine-year-old cook. 'She is a strong-headed one,' he says. 'And also the one that talks of hunger the most. My wife and I have gotten used to it, but the children still complain, and Livnes the most.'

Near the end of our visit, we manage to break down Livnes' resistance a little, even getting some laughs as we take silly photos of the children and show them to her on the camera screen. But as we walk away, we consider the difficult truth that Livnes and the other children have still many weeks of hunger ahead. Although Action Against Hunger and other NGOs are working with the government in this area to help as many households as possible, most families – most children like Livnes – will fall through the big holes in this patched-together safety net. As with Livnes' younger brother Krispin in 2005, seasonal hunger pushes millions of the youngest children to the brink of starvation every year, and

Figure 1.14   Livnes Banda, the daughter of Devison Banda, in Kasiya, Malawi.

Copyright © Bapu Vaitla.

permanently stunts the physical and cognitive development of tens of millions more.

The link between seasonality and malnutrition is often striking. Figure 1.15 shows how admissions and deaths of young children into the Nutritional Rehabilitation Unit of the local hospital near Kasiya follow a strongly seasonal pattern, peaking in the hunger months between December and March.

This seasonal pattern of malnutrition is not limited to Malawi, and neither is it a new phenomenon. Hunger season spikes in malnutrition occur all over the world, and have persisted for decades; Figure 1.16 is an example from northern Ghana during the late 1980s. In 1988, as every year, the annual harvest happened in September and October. By

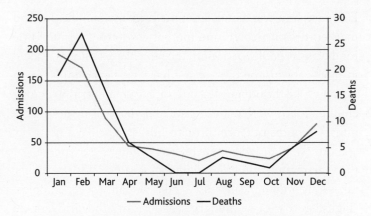

Figure 1.15 Admissions and deaths of children into NRU 2005–07,
St Andrews Hospital, Kasungu district, Malawi.

Source: St Andrews Hospital.

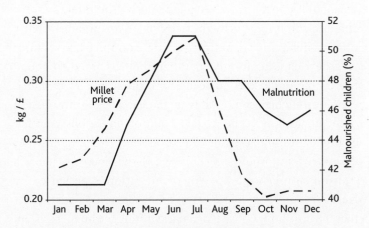

Figure 1.16 Seasonality in food prices and malnutrition in northern Ghana,
1988/89.

Source: Devereux (1992).

February, however, family granaries ran low, supplies in local markets became scarce, and food prices started to rise. Little food was available to eat until the next harvest. Prices peaked in June–July, just before the first harvest of early millet came in and broke the hunger season. Rates of malnutrition among children followed the same seasonal pattern, rising during the hungry months of April through July.

Note also that when millet prices fell in the second half of the year, malnutrition rates fell much more slowly – recovery takes longer than the increase, and is in reality never complete (Figure 1.16). Every hungry season is another irreversible setback to the development of children's physical strength and mental capacities.

Diseases also play a major role in creating or worsening seasonal cycles of malnutrition. Many of the world's worst illnesses, including diarrhoea, malaria and tuberculosis, are seasonally concentrated, brought on by the interaction of climatic conditions, growth cycles of vector organisms, and human behavioural patterns.[6] For example, cold winter weather leads to family members being forced to spend more time in close contact indoors, often in very cramped conditions, which can result in an increase in the transmission of tuberculosis and other acute respiratory infections. Another example is rainfall creating the pools of open stagnant water necessary for mosquito breeding, which then increases malaria transmission. The severity of malnutrition experienced by Devison's son Krispin in 2005 partially had to do with the fact that the little boy contracted malaria during the hunger season. When the timing of disease overlaps in this way with seasonal hunger, as happens commonly during the pre-harvest rainy season in many countries, the impact on health is devastating. Children weakened by hunger are more susceptible to illness, and those weakened by illness often have no appetite or are unable to absorb nutrients; such links between hunger and disease are insidious, and underappreciated. More so than any other single factor, hunger is responsible for weakening

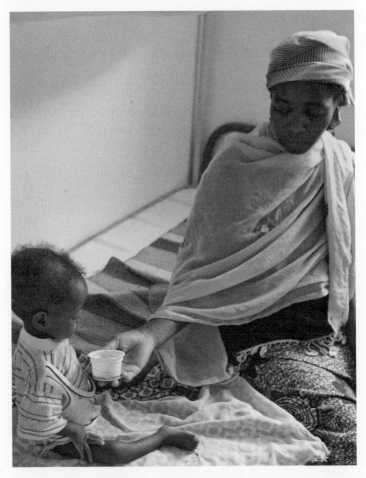

Figure 1.17 A mother encouraging her child to eat therapeutic food at a feeding centre in Keita, Niger.

immune systems and opening the door for killer epidemic diseases; it is estimated that the total burden of disease in poor countries could be reduced by nearly one-third if child malnutrition was eradicated.[7] Ending malnutrition would save the lives of several million young children every year who are killed by epidemic disease.[8]

Finally, the hunger season hurts children not only directly by reducing the household's food supply and increasing the burden of disease, but also indirectly through its effect on mothers. Nutritional deficiencies during pregnancy and breastfeeding can have irreversible developmental impacts on children.[9] Additionally, mothers in poor households often have to continue working during the hunger season, which leaves less time for child care. And when seasonal illnesses strike adults, the household's earning power is reduced, with consequences on food supply for the entire family.

THE FATHER OF FAMINE

If the response of governments and the international community to seasonal hunger has been sadly apathetic, one cannot say the same about famine events, which deservedly generate tremendous outrage and promises of 'never again'. Yet the irony is that famines *do* happen again and again, and this is so in part because an important truth is ignored: seasonal hunger is often the father of famine.[10] A brief look at the Malawian famine of 2002, in which at least 50,000 Malawians died of hunger and hunger-related causes – nine of whom, in Devison's recollection, were from Kasiya – illustrates this point.[11]

First, it is worth noting that what happens during the hunger season and what happens during famine differs only in severity. Looking again at the Malawi coping strategies graph (Figure 1.13(c) on page 25) shows this; the chart compares the responses of households in rural Malawi to a 'normal' hungry season in 1999 with their responses to the 2002 famine, the worst crisis in living memory. The sequence remained almost the same: for many poor households in rural Malawi (as in many other countries), every year is a food crisis, but some years are worse than others (the chart shows that many more Malawians were forced to resort to desperate measures, like asset sales and migration, during the famine year). Also significant is that borrowing did not increase much in 2002, and much less assistance from relatives and friends was secured than in the hungry season of 1999 – not because people did not ask for loans and food, but because this informal help was less available in 2002. Everyone was badly affected by the crisis and had nothing to spare for others.

But, in addition to the similarities in coping strategies during times of seasonal hunger and famine, the link between the two is causal. The year before the 2002 famine, drought caused a moderate collapse in the production of maize, Malawi's most important staple crop. About one-third less maize was produced in 2002 than in the previous year (which had been a bumper harvest), and this reduction is often blamed as the most important cause of the famine. Yet the 2002 harvest was actually *larger* than the average annual harvest of the ten-year period before the famine. In fact, per-capita maize availability was actually greater in the famine year than it was in 1992, 1994 and 1997, all years in which no famine occurred.[12] So what happened in 2002? The hunger of that year was deeper and deadlier for various reasons – among them poor management of the country's grain reserve, an issue we will look at later – but one of the major factors was that the past decade of suffering through annual cycles of seasonal hunger had stripped families of their resilience to crisis.

The decline of off-farm employment in preceding years was a key part of this eroding resilience. As we mentioned earlier, in Malawi many poor families seek work with better-off farmers in a casual labour contract called *ganyu*. Ganyu traditionally has been the most important source of money for the Malawian poor during the hunger season; it is a key coping strategy. But ganyu is disappearing. Figure 1.18, constructed through discussions with poor families in southern Malawi's Zomba district, shows the changes in ganyu sought and ganyu offered over the decade preceding the famine.

The graph makes it clear that ganyu availability began to decline a full four years before the 2002 famine actually

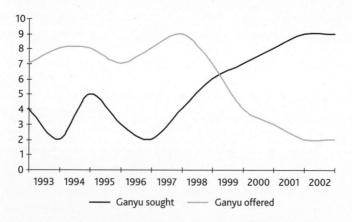

Figure 1.18   Ganyu sought and ganyu offered in rural Zomba district, Malawi. Values are given on a relative scale of 1 to 10, with 10 indicating the highest level of ganyu sought or offered.

Source: Devereux and Tiba (2007).

hit. With less and less ganyu, households lost income, sold assets, and generally began to exhaust their other coping strategies. What could have been a 'normal' hungry season in 2002 – what *should* have been a normal hungry season, given the size of the country's harvest – became, in the face of weakened resilience within communities and bad decisions within the corridors of power, one of the most terrible human catastrophes in recent memory.

The point is that famine cannot be stopped unless seasonal hunger is stopped. Famine is often the result of seasonal hunger being pushed to the point where whole economies and societies start to break down, and likewise seasonal hunger can be thought of as incipient famine. To draw a sharp contrast between the two is to invite complacency during the periods of seasonal hunger, when people are desperately struggling in less visible ways.

Moreover, as the Malawian-born anthropologist Elias Mandala argues in his book *The End of Chidyerano: A History of Food and Everyday Life in Malawi*, seasonal hunger has probably had a far more important role in determining the well-being of Malawi's people than the two or three famines that have occurred since the mid nineteenth century. As Mandala writes of one of his elderly informants living in the southern valleys of Malawi:

No one organised televised concerts for Mrs. Zachepa's children, who went to school without eating breakfast on a regular basis. Nor were they the primary concern of academics ... Mrs. Zachepa is talking about a deficit of a different order – recurrent hunger (*njala*) that kills its victims without attracting national or international attention. Mothers in particular know and lament this kind of hunger ...[13]

Devison Banda's story is not so different from that of Mrs Zachepa. Although it was the peak of the hunger season, Devison was able to chat with us about the weather as well as poverty. His daughter laughed at her photo instead of complaining about hunger. The visceral horror of famine was absent; but that does not mean there was not dying going on. It was a slower kind of dying, a quieter kind of violence, but it was there, and it deserves a response.

In the next chapter, we look at ideas that have indeed proven effective in responding to seasonal hunger, and argue for their implementation in those communities across the world, like Devison's village of Kasiya, that suffer from annual cycles of quiet starvation.

2
A World Full of Good Ideas

Figure 2.1 Coming home from the market carrying millet, in Guidan Koura, Niger.

Until recent times, seasonal cycles of surfeit and shortage were a part of the life of every human community. Anthropological accounts suggest that there were various means by which some pre-colonial African and Asian societies tried to dampen the impact of seasonal food shortages, including social arrangements to redistribute food and assets from rich to poor families (such as the *ganyu* employment in Malawi we discussed in the previous chapter).[1] Historical records from large civilisations, particularly from various Indian empires, suggest that some rulers created welfare and market intervention mechanisms to address hunger.[2]

Over centuries, many countries of the North developed mechanisms that reduced the risk of seasonal hunger: transport networks that allowed food to be shipped easily, sophisticated storage facilities, agricultural technologies that produced massive crop surpluses, and so on. The development of these mechanisms was fuelled by tremendous increases in wealth, a result of conquest, rapid scientific innovation, and, originally, sheer geographical luck.[3] The impacts of conquest and its associated evils – mass mortality from conflict and disease, slavery, expropriation of land and so on – on the food security of subjugated peoples were clearly immensely destructive. But even apart from these obvious forces, more subtle factors such as the imposition of European administrative structures and an increased focus on export cash cropping caused a quieter but often as ruinous disruption of traditional social and agricultural systems, leading to hunger and malnutrition.[4]

There are, however, also cases of imperial powers attempting to install anti-hunger systems in their colonies. The most famous example is probably the British creation of the Famine Codes in India, a set of guidelines developed by the various 'Famine Commissions', governmental bodies established to investigate the spectacular failures of the colonial regime in reacting to several catastrophic famines that devastated India following the imposition of British rule in 1858. Although the Codes were not fully implemented until the early decades of the twentieth century, they were in many ways the precursor of anti-hunger interventions as we know them today, emphasising large public works employment programmes, free relief to those unable to work, and the relaxation of taxes during times of impending famine.[5] The Codes were also innovative in that they recognised the seasonal pattern of hunger and food crises: when food prices rose more than 40 per cent above 'normal' for the time of year, this 'scarcity rate' was seen as a sign of potential famine, and led to activation of the Codes. The Famine Codes also represented an acceptance by those in power that they had a moral and legal duty to protect their poor and powerless citizens (or subjects) against the worst consequences of their poverty and vulnerability; by doing so, they introduced the idea that people receiving assistance were legal rights-holders, not simply fortunate beneficiaries. In addition to their positive attributes, however, the Famine Codes were also rightly criticised for focusing too narrowly on preventing starvation deaths while neglecting other forms of hunger. The Madras Code of 1905, for instance, stated that: 'though the State is bound to protect the people from starvation in times of distress, it is no part of its duty … to insure them against all suffering'.[6] The same sharp but ultimately false distinction between 'starvation prevention' and 'hunger prevention' prevails today, contributing to a situation wherein effective response to famine is seen as a question of global moral responsibility while the even greater sum of death and distress caused by seasonal hunger is largely ignored.[7]

In the first half of the twentieth century, however, the European powers did experiment in other colonies with various mechanisms for preventing seasonal hunger, including grain reserves, bans on food exports out of deficit areas, and price controls. These interventionist policies were motivated by evidence that markets were unable to guarantee food security, especially in poor rural areas with pronounced seasonality in agricultural production. In northern Ghana in the 1940s, for instance, the British colonial administration constructed seasonal grain reserves, which were stocked by buying locally-produced cereals in the harvest time for re-sale during the hungry season. The governmental Bulk Purchase and Storage Organisation that oversaw this programme stated two food security objectives that are still relevant to fighting seasonal hunger today: 'to show farmers that they need not be exploited by middlemen; [and] to store grain locally, instead of having to buy it back later in the season at inflated prices'.[8]

*   *   *

Building on these early initiatives, modern governments have experimented with a wide array of policies that have proven successful in the fight against seasonal hunger. Figure 2.2 illustrates what we believe are the best of these ideas – some of which have been practised for decades, others being more recent innovations – arranged into categories of 'emergency assistance', 'the social protection safety net' and 'agricultural livelihoods development'.

Emergency assistance measures are targeted at people who are suffering from seasonal hunger and need immediate help. The social protection safety net attempts to prevent families from falling into hunger in the first place, through a mix of employment, nutrition, price control and other policies.

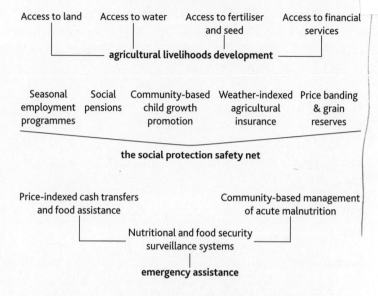

Figure 2.2 Intervention framework for fighting seasonal hunger.

Finally, agricultural livelihoods development initiatives focus on improving productivity through better access to key inputs, and thus try to work towards a future where rural households have high enough (and stable enough) incomes that the social protection safety net will rarely need to be accessed. Taken together, the group of ideas shown in Figure 2.2 represents a comprehensive intervention framework for fighting seasonal hunger. Let us look at each of these ideas in turn.

EMERGENCY ASSISTANCE

Nutrition and food security surveillance systems, cash/food transfers, and community-based management (CBM) of child malnutrition can work synergistically in emergency assistance efforts. Surveillance systems will identify who requires help and what interventions are needed; in the ideal scenario, the systems will be able to detect a deteriorating food security situation before malnutrition has become widespread. Early detection would then enable assistance in the form of cash and/or food transfers at the household level to help prevent malnutrition. If, however, the situation has already worsened to the point where severe acute malnutrition[*] is at high levels, then CBM efforts can provide broad and effective nutritional treatment coverage.

Nutritional and Food Security Surveillance

Historically, the vast majority of people affected by seasonal hunger have gone unnoticed by their national health systems and international agencies alike. Victims of seasonal hunger do not make the front-page headlines, and as a result many fall gravely ill, and some die. In recent years, however, new surveillance system approaches have improved our understanding of when and where seasonal hunger and malnutrition occur. In Malawi, a surveillance system run by the government and supported by Action Against Hunger provides month-by-month information from every region of the country.

The Malawi surveillance system has nutritional and food security components. The nutritional component monitors weight and height trends in a sample of preschool children attending government growth monitoring clinics. Each group of children is followed for twelve consecutive months to assess

---

[*] Severe acute malnutrition is a dangerous kind of malnutrition that is caused by recent drastic reductions in nutrient intake. It can result from either a decline in food consumption itself or the inability of the body to absorb or retain consumed nutrients, for example due to illness. Untreated, severe acute malnutrition will lead to irreparable damage to cognitive and physical development, and eventually to death.

Figure 2.3   Child being weighed in bi-weekly growth monitoring for
nutritional surveillance, Mchinji District, Malawi.

seasonal changes in their nutritional status. Although the
system follows only a small sample of children, the results are
indicative of nutritional trends in all parts of the country.

From this group of children, the system selects a further sub-
sample to survey their family's food security status. A baseline
survey gathers basic information: demographic data, assets
owned, types of agricultural system, sources of income, access
to water and sanitation, and so on. Monthly repeat surveys
then assess changes in cash income and food consumption
flows and combine the information into a composite 'Food
Stress Index' (FSI; see Box 2.1 for the eight variables included
in the index). The FSI ranges on a scale between 0 and 100,
with 100 being the worst score possible.[9]

The FSI for Malawi as a whole for the 2003–06 period
is given in Figure 2.4. One can see clear seasonal 'humps'

Box 2.1   Variables Measured in the Food Stress Index

1. The percentage of households that have very low supplies of starch staple food: less than 20kg of maize, dry cassava or other cereal, and no cassava or sweet potato ready for harvest.
2. The percentage of households that have a potential shortage in the longer term: less than 50kg of maize, dry cassava or other cereal, and no cassava or sweet potato ready for harvest in the next two months.
3. The percentage of households with income less than MK1,000 (£3.66) per month.
4. The percentage of households having difficulty finding *ganyu* employment.
5. The percentage of households eating three meals a day.
6. The percentage of households not eating groundnuts or legumes on the previous day.
7. The percentage of households reporting they did not have enough food at some time in the month.
8. The percentage of households going whole days without eating a staple food.

in food stress in each of the three years, and also that the seasonal hunger of 2005/06 was far worse than in the preceding years.

The purpose of the surveillance system is to inform policymakers when and to what degree the food situation is deteriorating. Evidence of an impending serious situation will compel a more detailed nutritional and food security investigation, followed by assistance response. Although the surveillance system covers only a small sample of children and families, it is a vast improvement over current nutritional and food security assessments that characterise situations at only one given point of time. If that chosen point of time happens to be inaccurate – and one can see from Figure 2.4

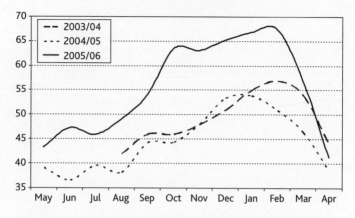

Figure 2.4   Food Stress Index, Malawi, 2003/04 to 2005/06 seasons.

Source: Action Against Hunger-Malawi.

that while the existence of a hunger season is predictable, the exact timing of the peak of the season varies from year to year, depending on trends in rainfall and prices – then policy and programme responses will also be faulty and families may go hungry when more accurate information could have led to preventative interventions. In short, current methods of nutritional and food security assessment are like a photo snapshot, whereas a surveillance system is like a motion picture. Warning signs of impending crisis are more easily noticed in the latter.

Price-Indexed Cash Transfers and Food Assistance

Providing food directly – 'food aid' – has traditionally been the dominant form of assistance sent to people suffering from hunger. In the past decade, however, assistance in the form of money – 'cash transfers' – has become increasingly popular as an alternative to food aid, especially in Africa. The advantages of cash are many. Cash gives people more choices than food, enabling them to meet a range of food and non-food needs, including health expenses, clothing, and – even in emergency situations – the purchasing of livestock and other key assets needed to build livelihoods.[10] Cash also has 'multiplier effects' in the economy: spending cash transfers will generate income and employment for others. Cash can help farmers invest in their production systems and thus stimulate local food economies, whereas food aid can put local traders out of business and undermine incentives for farmers to produce more food.

However, there are particular concerns with the use of cash. Perhaps the most serious problems occur when seasonal price spikes reduce the amount of food that a given amount of cash can buy, or when market supplies of food are inadequate to meet the demand generated by cash transfers. In Malawi, the 'Food and Cash Transfers' project (FACT) and 'Dowa Emergency Cash Transfers' project (DECT), implemented by the NGO Concern Worldwide as assistance to thousands of drought-affected farmers in 2006 and 2007, tried to respond to these problems. The FACT project provided a monthly food package (maize, beans and oil), plus enough cash to buy the same package again in local markets, for four months during the 2005/06 hungry season, a year when bad weather caused a national maize shortage and the President of Malawi declared a 'state of disaster'. The food package was provided in case lack of supplies in local markets left people unable to buy food with their cash transfers. The DECT project, meanwhile, delivered only cash transfers during the 2007 hungry season, in a year when there was a bumper harvest at national level – so there was no problem with food supplies – but erratic rainfall caused localised crop failure in two districts. An innovative feature of both FACT and DECT was that local food markets were monitored continuously throughout the hungry season and the amount of cash transferred to families was adjusted as food prices rose or fell, to ensure that people had access to adequate quantities of maize, beans and cooking oil at whatever price prevailed. This meant that people were fully compensated for seasonal price rises, which were significant – for example, the price of maize doubled between January and March 2006 – but the cost of this price seasonality was underwritten by the project implementers, rather than by poor families themselves.

As long as markets are able to supply adequate amounts of food in response to greater demand, this strategy of 'indexing' the amount of cash transferred to food prices can be very effective. If food markets are not functioning well, external infusions of food should be considered in conjunction with price-indexed cash transfers. Even in the latter case, however, food used in assistance efforts should be procured from as nearby as possible. Usually, surplus food can be purchased from national or regional markets, saving considerably on the time and monetary cost of transporting food across oceans from donor countries; the price of transport presently comprises a significant portion of total food aid budgets.[11] Food aid from rich countries should only be used in the rare situations when it is the quickest and most cost-effective way to deliver assistance.

Community-Based Management of Acute Malnutrition

The community-based management (CBM) approach is revolutionising the treatment of malnutrition. Traditionally, children suffering from severe acute malnutrition are treated in hospital-type inpatient settings. Per-patient costs and staffing needs for this approach, however, are very high; as a result, only a limited number of malnourished children are fortunate enough to receive treatment. The CBM approach addresses these issues by mobilising communities themselves to treat the 80 per cent or so of malnourished children who do not have other illnesses or complications.[12] The use of easy to administer therapeutic foods and the periodic support of health professionals makes this community-based strategy viable. Meanwhile, inpatient care in Therapeutic Feeding Centres (TFCs) can concentrate on the remaining 20 per cent of malnourished children who do have complications.

The first step in CBM is to identify sick children through 'active case-finding', wherein health workers or the community itself screen children for malnutrition on a regular basis. Case-finding is facilitated by easy-to-use malnutrition diagnosis approaches such as measuring mid-upper arm circumference. Active case-finding not only leads to more malnourished children in the community being identified, but also to earlier diagnosis of symptoms, which will increase the recovery rate during treatment.

After case-finding, health professionals determine whether a child has complications. If the child does have complications, he or she is referred to an inpatient facility for closely managed therapeutic feeding. However, if the child has no complications, families themselves treat malnourished children at home, with the support of a weekly check-up by trained health staff. The use of nutrient-dense Ready-to-Use Foods (RUFs), a recent innovation in nutritional treatment technology, is the key to this home-based approach. The peanut and milk-based RUFs do not require preparation, store well, are not prone to bacterial contamination, and are easy to feed to children above six months old.[13] In addition, RUFs can often be produced locally at a low cost, providing a boost to the community economy.

Figure 2.5 Mother assisting her severely acutely malnourished child to eat therapeutic food, St Andrews Hospital, near Kasungu, Malawi.

Finally, the CBM approach is simple enough that the strategy can be applied not only for emergency treatment, but also for preventative purposes in an at-risk population – for example, among children that have been identified as moderately malnourished but have not yet become severely malnourished. The CBM approach may even allow blanket coverage for all children in a community entering the hunger season;[14] in this way, RUFs can be integrated into child growth promotion efforts, a key part of the social protection safety net we discuss later.

Thus, in its ideal form, the CBM approach rests on five pillars: community and frontline health worker case-finding of malnutrition using rapid diagnosis approaches; inpatient therapeutic feeding centres for malnourished children *with* complications; home-based therapeutic programmes for malnourished children *without* complications; local production of RUFs; and supplementary feeding for prevention of severe acute malnutrition.

Although CBM approaches have been tested on a large scale for only a few years, the results have thus far been impressive. In a survey of 21 CBM programmes in Malawi, Ethiopia and Sudan between 2001 and 2005, coverage (the percentage of the total child population screened and treated for malnutrition) increased almost fivefold over traditional treatment approaches; overall, nearly three-quarters of all children in the project areas were included in the screening. Four out of five children who were treated through CBM recovered, a rate that compares favourably to inpatient care.[15] There is reason to be optimistic that the coverage and recovery rates will improve even more as CBM methods are refined.

Statistics like these, however, do not fully capture the implications of scaling-up CBM globally. Nynke Nutma, a nutritionist and health specialist working for Action Against Hunger in Malawi, spoke to us about the potential impact of CBM on her work. 'If most of the cases are treated in the community, you can focus in the inpatient centre on those children who really need help,' she tells us. 'But [without CBM], to try and treat one hundred children with two nurses in the inpatient feeding centres, it's impossible. I remember times when I was just too tired to keep going, I had to go home, and then I came back the next day to find that the child I had stopped at the evening before had died during the night.' Under community-based management, children do not have to die for preventable reasons like staff shortage. Universal screening and treatment for acute malnutrition – care for all children who need it – can be a realistic goal.

THE SOCIAL PROTECTION SAFETY NET

Although effective implementation of emergency programmes is critical to save lives in the hunger season, a preventative social protection safety net can reduce the need for those emergency interventions in the first place. For people who are able to work, seasonal employment programmes that pay wages indexed to food prices are the best way for this safety net to deliver resources to families. For people who are restricted in their ability to work, particularly the elderly, cash transfers could be provided in the form of 'social pensions'. Since this latter group is unable to work at any time of the year, pensions should be provided year-round, but again should be indexed to food prices so that pensioners can afford an adequate diet in all seasons.

In addition to assisting households and pensioners, there should be a social protection safety net component that focuses directly on mothers and children. We suggest that community-based growth promotion initiatives, which offer an integrated set of health and nutrition services rooted at the village level, are the best approach to protecting these groups. Again, although the growth promotion services should be available year-round, benefits – particularly the supplementary feeding component – should increase during the hunger season, in response to lower household food availability and higher food prices.

The section below also discusses the idea of weather-indexed agricultural insurance, a way to protect farmers against the weather shocks that can severely damage farm livelihoods. Finally, price banding policies – setting a 'floor' price for farmers and 'ceiling' prices for food buyers – are also valuable components of a social protection safety net, and can be linked to national grain reserves.

Seasonal Employment Programmes

Seasonal employment programmes have their roots in the massive public works initiatives of the Great Depression of the 1930s. Since that time, rich and poor countries alike have periodically provided temporary public sector employment as a means to both ease poverty and create needed infra-structure. India, China and Bangladesh all have large long-standing seasonal employment programmes, and many African countries have implemented sizable programmes of their own in the past two decades.[16] Ethiopia's Productive Safety Nets Programme (PSNP) is currently the largest seasonal employment initiative in Africa, reaching over 8 million people during the hunger season every year.

Seasonal employment programmes meet several needs. Labour power is often the only resource over which poor families, and particularly landless families, have control. Employment programmes allow these families the opportunity to convert labour into cash and food during times of the year when jobs are scarce. In addition, the assets created by seasonal employment labour often directly address the problems of seasonality: for example, drainage systems decrease the threat of malaria and diarrhoea, all-weather roads allow access to markets and health care facilities in the rainy season, and soil conservation structures help to increase agricultural productivity.

In Guidan Koura in Niger – the home village of Zara, whom we met in the previous chapter – Action Against Hunger runs a seasonal 'Cash-for-Work' employment programme. An increasing population and lack of alternatives for wood

Figure 2.6   Cash-for-Work programme near Guidan Koura, in Niger.

and fodder have led to widespread deforestation in the area around Guidan Koura. Without trees and other vegetation to hold the soil in place, erosion from the harsh winds has turned the hills into stony deserts where little grows. The community members have thus decided to use the Cash-for-Work programme to reforest these hills to slow down erosion. The task is difficult – the workers have to excavate a half-metre deep hole in hard, stony soil to plant each sapling – but well worth the benefits.

The work is for the future: to grow a forest. But the gains are felt in the present as well; coming as it does in the hunger season, the income received by the workers is critical. Over half will be spent on food, and the rest on other essential needs (Figure 2.7).

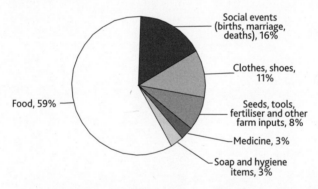

Figure 2.7   Intended utilisation of income gained through Action Against Hunger Cash-for-Work project. From discussion with women workers, Guidan Koura village, Niger.

The choice of wage type, cash or food, is a critical decision when designing employment programmes. Indexing cash wages to food prices in the manner of the FACT and DECT programmes in Malawi described earlier, as well as injecting food as needed to increase supplies in local markets, is one way to address the issue. A complementary strategy is to provide, season by season, a menu of choices for participants themselves to choose how they would like to be paid; discussions with participants in another employment programme in Malawi found that farming families would prefer different types of payment at different times of the year. During the hungry season when food is scarce and expensive, food-for-work was chosen by most families (indexed cash wages were not an option in this survey). Around harvest time, when food is plentiful, most chose cash-for-work as a means of meeting their non-food expenses. At planting time, families were inclined towards yet another option: inputs-for-work – wages paid in the form of fertiliser and seed. As far as we know, this type of seasonally differentiated payment schedule for employment programmes has not been implemented anywhere in the world, but it merits a deeper look, not only for its ability to provide the 'right' type of wage, but also because of its participatory nature: it puts the people served by the intervention in control of its design.

India's National Rural Employment Guarantee Scheme (NREGS) is the newest major employment initiative. NREGS is unlike its predecessors in one critical way: it guarantees households a legal right to request 100 days of employment a year at the minimum wage from the government. These 100 days can be demanded during any time of the year, depending on when households experience a shortfall in job opportunities and income.[17] If employment is not provided promptly by the state, families are entitled to an employment allowance. NREGS' transformation of employment from 'provided benefit' to 'legal entitlement' is subtle but revolutionary, and we discuss the programme in more detail in the next chapter.

Social Pensions

A particular form of cash transfer is spreading across southern Africa: 'social pensions', or regular cash transfers to elderly citizens. South Africa first implemented social pensions in the 1920s, but it was not until the 1970s that they were adopted by Namibia, and even more recently by Botswana (in 1996), Lesotho (in 2004) and Swaziland (in 2005). Although the pensions are not solely intended to address seasonal hunger, their impact on all forms of poverty and food insecurity is enormous, and they offer many lessons for the design and implementation of effective anti-hunger programmes elsewhere.

Social pensions are not the same as standard pensions. Standard pensions are usually paid to workers when they retire from formal employment and are funded by contributions, linked to pre-retirement income, made by both employers and employees. Social pensions, in contrast, are given by the state as an unconditional cash transfer to all elderly citizens (or in some cases only to poor elderly citizens), with 60 or 65 years old as the most common age threshold. A key feature of social pensions is that they are a legal right that can be claimed by all elderly citizens, not 'discretionary' or targeted assistance that is given to some but not others and can be withdrawn at any time. This 'legal entitlement' aspect of social pensions provides a basis for political mobilisation when the right is violated. For example, in November 2006, when delays and errors in pension lists caused thousands of social pensioners at risk of hunger in Swaziland to return home empty-handed after queuing all day, Members of Parliament representing their affected constituents stridently took up the issue. The MPs' action resulted in swift governmental response to resolve the problem. In standard development programmes not based on legal entitlements, such examples of rapid governmental response to problems are rare.

The social pension becomes especially crucial in the hungry season and bad years. During the southern African drought of 1992, social pensions in Namibia saved numerous lives. At the onset of the emergency, the government included elderly people on its list of 'vulnerable groups' eligible for food aid, but then recognised that recipients of the monthly social pension were actually among the least vulnerable of rural Namibians. Pensioners were in fact overwhelmed with requests for assistance from relatives and neighbours, and most tried to help as much as they could. For the duration of the food crisis, many children were sent to stay with older relatives who were receiving the social pension; Gertrude, one grandmother we met in western Namibia, looked after no fewer than eleven grandchildren in 1992. Pensioners became the sole source of access to food in many poor communities, often to the point of overstretching their resources.[18] The impact of pensions on families' well-being during the 1992 drought is shown by looking again at the first two diagrams of the coping strategies graph we first saw in Chapter 1 (see Figures 1.13(a) and (b) on page 24).

Ethiopia in 2006 experienced good rainfall, but food rationing during the hungry season was very high. Among the nearly 1,000 poor households interviewed, almost four in five cut back on their food consumption, signifying that seasonal hunger is a feature of 'normal' life in the rural highlands of Ethiopia. In contrast, the 1992 southern Africa drought was catastrophic in severity, affecting 20 million people and killing more than a million cattle across the region. But fewer Namibian families rationed food in 1992 than in Ethiopia in 2006, partly because the Government of Namibia launched a prompt and effective Drought Relief Programme, and partly because the government's social pension system provided a guaranteed monthly income to all citizens over 60 throughout the crisis period. These pensions enabled even the poorest families to buy enough food to survive.

Like cash and food transfer programmes, social pensions should also be indexed to price changes. Most social pensions currently in existence are adjusted only occasionally to keep up with inflation, and none that we are aware of takes into account seasonal or other fluctuations in food prices. So the real value of the pension might well be lowest when it is needed most – during a food crisis. We argue that social pensions should instead be indexed to reflect rising prices of basic goods, including seasonal fluctuations in food prices.

Finally, it should be noted that pensions could extend beyond the elderly to encompass other groups unable to work – people with disabilities,[19] the labour-constrained (e.g. widows looking after young children), and so on.

Community-Based Child Growth Promotion

Community-based child growth promotion programmes protect preschool children and pregnant/lactating mothers from hunger by integrating a wide variety of health and nutrition services at the village level. The overall objective of growth promotion programmes is to assure optimal nutrition during the most important child growth periods – during pregnancy and in the first years of life. Seasonal patterns of food deficit or disease that interrupt these critical periods can have permanent developmental consequences. The services commonly found in growth promotion programmes include: child growth monitoring; antenatal care; breastfeeding promotion; health, hygiene and nutrition education; and supplementary feeding of pregnant women, lactating mothers and preschool children.

Child growth monitoring takes nutritional surveillance a step further by putting into place systems that measure the growth of every child, not just a sub-sample. Village-level workers, who can establish personal relationships with local families in a way that outsiders cannot, are critical to making such a universal coverage strategy work.

The health of women during pregnancy is an especially important determinant of a child's future nutritional status. This is starkly illustrated by the case of India: despite the country's relatively lower levels of income poverty, India has very high child malnutrition rates compared to Sub-Saharan Africa, and the difference is thought to be primarily a result of maternal nutritional deficiency. In India, over one-third of women have a below-normal Body Mass Index (BMI; weight in relation to height) and nearly three-fifths are anaemic. Largely as a result of their mother's poor nutritional status, over 40 per cent of Indian children are born underweight.[20] Providing supplementary food to pregnant women, and increasing the amount provided during the hunger season, will help to reduce this 'inter-generational' malnutrition, and thus have positive consequences that last for a child's lifetime.

Given the importance of breast milk as a source of food during the first two years of a child's life, protecting the nutritional status of lactating mothers is also critical to child health. Energy and nutrient requirements during pregnancy are elevated, and deficits that occur during the hunger season – worsened by the fact that many poor pregnant women have

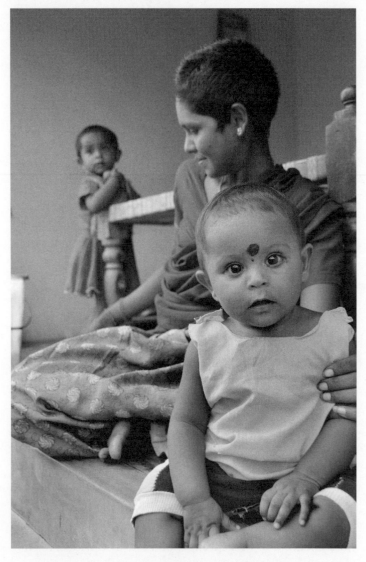

Figure 2.8   Mother with child at growth promotion centre in
Annapanenivari Gudem, Andhra Pradesh, India.

Copyright © E. Whelan.

to continue working in these months to earn income and buy food – can have damaging consequences on maternal and child health. Again, supplementary feeding programmes should adjust the amount of food given to lactating mothers depending on the season.

After six months of age, supplementary feeding programmes can also target children themselves. While many programmes in the past have focused on feeding children in schools as an incentive to increase enrolment and improve academic performance, for nutritional purposes it is even more important to concentrate programmes on the 0–2 year age group. The first two years of life are absolutely critical for establishing a normal growth pattern; children who are malnourished in this initial period cannot catch up in subsequent years. In addition, over two-thirds of child deaths worldwide occur during the first year of life, and the majority of these are associated with malnutrition.[21] It is especially critical to ensure that these children are fulfilling their nutritional requirements during the lean season.

Supplementary feeding programmes tend to concentrate on providing calories and protein, but it is important to consider micronutrient sufficiency as well. Millions of children a year are victims of micronutrient deficiencies, especially of vitamin A, iron and iodine. The consequences of micronutrient deficiency are serious, ranging from mental retardation to blindness to death. Provision of micronutrient supplements can save children from these outcomes, and is in fact one of the most cost-effective development interventions of any kind for improving human health.[22] One of the major challenges in providing micronutrient supplements is establishing an effective delivery mechanism: capsules have to be taken regularly, in the case of iron at least once a week. Incorporating micronutrient supplementation in a community-based growth promotion structure can assist in overcoming these delivery issues.

A recent survey of 15 community growth promotion and similar child health/nutrition programmes worldwide concludes that, given the presence of certain contextual and programme 'success factors',[23] malnutrition is considerably reduced among enrolled children: independent of other factors, the best growth promotion programmes lower malnutrition by one to two percentage points a year.[24] This rate of impact worldwide would equate to several million preschool children being prevented from falling into malnutrition every year.

Weather-Indexed Agricultural Insurance Schemes

Because agriculture is so risky, farmers need insurance against harvest failure. But crop insurance is generally not available to poor farmers in Africa and Asia, for various reasons: because insurance markets are weakly developed, because a problem like drought affects so many farmers that insurance companies will be unable to pay all the claimants, and because the premiums are often too high for poor farmers to afford. For these reasons, previous attempts to extend crop insurance to small farmers in the 1960s and 1970s failed.

Now, however, an innovative 'weather-indexing' approach to agricultural insurance is being pilot tested in India, Ethiopia, Malawi and other countries. In these schemes, participating farmers are paid out if rainfall in their district falls below a certain percentage of the long-term average; the lower the rainfall, the higher the payout. This payout is intended to compensate farmers for lost food production and income from crop sales, ensuring that they can purchase enough food to feed their family until the next harvest.

From the insurer's point of view, there are two advantages to this crop insurance idea. The first is that farms do not need to be individually assessed following a drought, which greatly reduces administrative costs for the insurer. Secondly, farmers have no incentive to work less and claim on their insurance when the harvest fails – a major worry of insurers in the past – because assessments are made for rainfall at the district level, not the farm level. From the farmer's point of view, 'weather-indexed insurance' offers exactly the kind of guaranteed safety net that they need to survive bad years, and could give them the confidence to take moderate risks such as investing in fertiliser or high-yielding seed varieties.

Of course, the problem of costly premiums for poor farmers persists with this 'weather-indexing' idea, as does the risk of major payouts for the insurance company. For these reasons, financial support from governments or donors might be required.[25] But the costs of supporting an insurance programme must be weighed against the costs of providing humanitarian assistance once a crisis has started.

Price Banding and Strategic Grain Reserves

After independence from colonial powers, many governments established agricultural marketing boards, which had a mandate to support farmers and ensure national food security. Governments believed that weak markets and exploitative traders exposed poor farmers and consumers to great risk, and these 'parastatal' marketing boards were to be the first line of defence. The parastatals sold fertiliser and seeds at subsidised prices to ensure that poor farmers had affordable access to these agricultural inputs. They then purchased harvest surpluses at a fixed minimum price (the 'floor' price) from all areas of the country to guarantee a fair income for all farmers. The harvest was stored in national 'Strategic Grain Reserves'. The grain reserves not only provided a buffer stock in case of emergencies, but were also used to fight seasonal hunger. The grain was stored until the hunger season and then sold at a fixed cheap price (the 'ceiling' price) to all consumers, boosting access to food and fighting price increases in the market. The two practices of buying food at a floor price to help farmers and selling it at a ceiling price to help consumers are together called 'price banding'.

Despite their vitally important mandate, in many countries the actual functioning of price banding systems was far from perfect. Parastatals were rightly criticised for being expensive and inefficient, frequently corrupt, and for interfering with the development of the private sector. While defenders argued that parastatals were needed because markets were weak, critics complained that markets were weak because of unfair competition from parastatals. Where private traders were either banned or absent, farmers risked being locked into relationships with parastatal marketing boards on terms they could not control. Often, they did not receive the promised agricultural inputs on time, they had limited choice in what they could buy or sell, and they were paid late (and often under-paid) for their produce.

In the 1980s, the pendulum in the global 'state versus market' policy debate swung sharply to the right, and donor countries and agencies applied conditions to their loans and grants that forced governments of poor countries to withdraw agricultural subsidies and remove controls over crop and food prices. The hope was that freeing markets from the 'dead hand' of state regulation would stimulate agricultural production and trade, leading to rapid economic growth and poverty reduction. Under pressure from powerful agencies such as the World Bank and International Monetary Fund (IMF), most of Africa's agricultural parastatals were closed, scaled down, or commercialised.

Unfortunately, this often created more problems than it solved. Like many other parastatals, Malawi's Agricultural Development and Marketing Corporation (ADMARC) closed its loss-making 'social marketing' depots, those food purchase/sales centres that were mostly located in deep rural communities, where food insecurity was highest but incomes were lowest. This meant that thousands of farmers who had come to rely on ADMARC to sell them inputs at planting time, to buy their crops at harvest time, and to sell them food in the hungry season no longer had access to their 'buyer and seller of last resort'. The expectation of those who advocated market liberalisation was that the private sector would rush in to fill the gap vacated by ADMARC. Instead, there was a vacuum; no traders came to these isolated villages. Previously, ADMARC had subsidised its loss-making depots using the money it made from more profitable depots elsewhere. But private traders have no incentive to do this, and few saw any profit in travelling for hours across difficult countryside to buy or sell a few bags of maize to a few households in a tiny village, when the big towns near main roads offered easier access and much larger, more reliable and more affluent markets.

But perhaps the most damaging reform in terms of food security in Malawi was a requirement that the Strategic Grain Reserve should be operated on a 'cost recovery' basis. This meant that the government parastatal in charge of the reserve, the National Food Reserve Agency (NFRA), was instructed to take commercial loans to buy its stock, and had to cover its costs by buying and selling maize on the open market. In 1999 the NFRA took a loan of £15 million from a South African bank to stock the grain reserve to full capacity (180,000 metric tonnes). Following two bumper harvests, the grain reserve was starting to rot and the NFRA's debt had risen to £16.5 million. So in 2001 the International Monetary Fund advised the government to sell the old stock and use the proceeds to repay the debt, and then replenish the reserve by buying fresh maize after the next harvest. Accordingly, the NFRA silos were emptied, with most of the maize being exported to neighbouring countries. But then the food crisis of 2002 struck – and the national grain reserve was empty, leaving the government unable to prevent famine. This experience exposed the paradox of trying to operate an agency with a food security mandate on a cost-recovery basis: instead of recycling stock every year, the NFRA held on to maize waiting for prices to rise, so it could sell at a price that would allow the loan to be repaid.

Northern donors have spent much of the last three decades pressuring the governments of poor countries to dismantle interventionist strategies like price banding. Is this the right direction? Were past price banding efforts by governments to protect their poorest citizens against seasonal hunger and famine bad ideas that deserved to be thrown out? Or were they good ideas but badly implemented and too expensive for poor countries? It is certainly true that parastatals and subsidies had their problems, and we are not arguing for a carbon-copy resuscitation of policies and institutions that have failed. But history teaches us that seasonal hunger cannot be addressed without protecting the poor from volatile prices. We argue that in view of the ongoing crises in small farm agriculture and food grain markets, price banding – with much stronger in-built anti-corruption and performance checks – deserves another look.

AGRICULTURAL LIVELIHOODS DEVELOPMENT

A strong social protection safety net is essential in the fight against seasonal hunger, but a permanent victory can only come about if agricultural productivity is increased. This is obviously the case for poor families that depend on farming as their income source, but also for landless families that depend on agricultural labour work: increased on-farm productivity can translate into higher rural growth and, in the right policy environment, more job opportunities for wage workers.

Investment in agriculture has been an on-again, off-again priority over the decades, following dominant ideological trends. The 1980s and 1990s saw large decreases in public investment into agriculture; partially as a result, productivity has slowed down. The ongoing global food price crisis, however, has again pushed agriculture to the centre of the political conversation about hunger. The key to increasing productivity lies in increased investment into agricultural research and training on one side and improved access to inputs on the other, especially land, water, fertiliser, seed, and financial services. It is this latter set of considerations, access to inputs, on which we focus in the sections below.

Land

Land is the most fundamental of all inputs required for farming. In many places where seasonal hunger and risks of famine are highest, including southern Malawi and highland Ethiopia, access to land is severely limited. Many farmers are struggling to survive from fields so small they are sometimes called 'starvation plots', and many other families are completely landless.

There are two competing lines of thought on the links between land access and agricultural productivity. One is that agricultural development policy should not purposefully strive to guarantee land access to poor families, and instead should allow a process of land consolidation to occur – large farmers becoming larger by buying out smaller, less competitive farmers, as has happened (and continues to happen) in many Northern countries. The contention is that large, consolidated farms can be more productive than small farms, capitalising on economies of scale through mechanisation and other improved technologies. In addition, large landholders can more easily absorb price and climate shocks, and are likely to have better access to credit as a result (moneylenders will see them as less risky investments). Credit will then allow even more investment into yield-enhancing technology, kick-starting a cycle of ever-higher productivity.

Others argue the opposite: that productivity is generally higher on small farms. This is mainly due to two factors: greater input use and the 'incentive' effect. Per-unit area, small farmers generally invest more fertiliser, water and labour into their fields, which leads to higher yields. The incentive effect refers to the fact that small farms often use only household labour to run the farm operations, while large farms generally need to hire outside labour. Because household members have a greater stake in increased agricultural productivity than do hired workers, the impact of household labour is generally higher than hired labour.

Both lines of argument have mountains of evidence supporting their claims, although the majority of rural development-focused academics have tended to support the latter 'small farms are more productive' contention.[26] In practice, the conditions surrounding agriculture – whether small farmers have access to affordable credit, whether input subsidies are available, whether technology appropriate for small farms is available, and so on – determine which strategy is likely to produce the greatest gains in productivity.

Of course, the purpose of facilitating access to land is not just to increase agricultural productivity in the country as a whole, but also to reduce hunger among the rural poor through providing a critical livelihood resource. For this reason, many governments in Africa and Asia – even those that simultaneously promote some degree of land consolidation, particularly for export cropping purposes – have employed a variety of land reform strategies to increase poor families' access to land. These include straightforward expropriation and redistribution of rich farmers' land, as in Cuba, China and Ethiopia; the creation of 'land ceiling' laws like India's, under which individuals can only own a fixed amount of land, with the excess parcels purchased by the state and redistributed to poorer families; and 'willing seller, willing buyer' models like that of South Africa, wherein the government purchases land at market rates from landowners and then assists landless families with grants and loans to purchase the land. As can be imagined, the ideological environment determines which form of land redistribution is exercised. In many countries, powerful rural elites make forcible land reform politically impossible. In others, including South Africa, the glacial pace of market-based land reform is leading to rising resentment among the rural landless.[27]

A more moderate approach to improving land access is to concentrate on improving the legal and administrative framework around land ownership and tenure. Often, rural families have only customary, not legal, title to land they have used for generations. Without official title, powerful interests can forcefully push families off their land. Improvement of the legal and administrative framework can prevent such expulsions from occurring, and also provide a basis for legal challenge if they do occur. Similar legal protections can prevent sharecroppers and renters of land from suffering exploitative terms of lease. This focus on linking poor families to a responsive and efficient legal and administrative structure has generally been the favoured approach of major donor institutions, especially the World Bank, to improving land access for the rural poor.[28]

Land access is an extremely delicate political issue. But the links between land ownership, poverty and hunger among rural people are clear and undeniable, and action on improving land access for poor families lies at the heart of fighting hunger, especially in the face of widespread unemployment in many rural economies.

Water

The availability of water is central to preventing seasonal cycles of hunger. Irrigation can make the difference between one harvest and two, between half a year of hunger and no hunger at all. Presently, only 5 per cent of farmland in Sub-Saharan Africa and one-third in Asia is irrigated.[29] In some countries, including Ethiopia, vast amounts of untapped groundwater and surface water exist, but significant investment will be required to build the infrastructure needed to harvest this water. In other countries, groundwater tables are rapidly being depleted, and access of poor families to more water can only occur if efficiency of current use, through drip irrigation and other technologies, is improved.

In addition, climate change is likely to intensify water problems in the coming decades, in two ways: by reducing total rainfall and by causing rainfall to become more erratic and unpredictable, with a higher frequency of extreme weather events like droughts and floods. The rainfall pattern over the last two decades in Ethiopia illustrates both of these problems, an overall drop and higher year-to-year variability (see Figure 2.9). Climatologists argue that a strong link exists between these trends and climate change.[30]

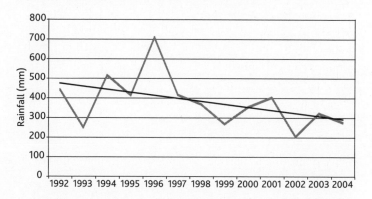

Figure 2.9   Rainfall during the long rainy (meher) season, Aposto village, Ethiopia. Linear trendline shown in black. From Ethiopian Meteorological Services Agency.[31]

The increasing unpredictability of rainfall distribution *within* a growing season is also of concern. Many food crises have occurred when harvests failed despite total annual rainfall being more than sufficient, but poorly distributed over the crop cycle; for example, in northern Namibia in 1992 a three-week break in the rains was enough to wither the maize crop in farmers' fields and cause a devastating 'agricultural drought', even though precipitation for the entire season was higher than the five-year average.[32] Overall, most studies looking at the future potential impact of climate change predict that Africa will face rising water stress and falling cereal yields, with some countries, including the extremely food-insecure nations of Chad, Niger and Zambia, at risk of losing virtually all of their arable land by 2100.[33]

In this challenging environment of falling groundwater tables and increasingly unreliable rainfall, improved water management is crucial. Public works and rural infrastructure programmes should concentrate on soil and water conservation activities that are appropriate and effective to each local context. As suggested by the UN's International Fund for Agricultural Development (IFAD), a 'Blue Revolution' is needed to focus policy attention on the availability and efficient use of water, particularly in Sub-Saharan Africa.[34]

Fertiliser and Seed

As we mentioned earlier, many measures implemented under agricultural liberalisation reforms in the 1980s and 1990s had the effect of reducing the access of poor farmers to fertiliser and seeds, which in many countries became unaffordable for everyone except large-scale commercial farmers. Poor farmers also owned fewer animals, so they had little or no access to organic manure to replace the fertiliser. As a result, soil nutrients were depleted with each succeeding crop, yields on small family farms fell, and the hunger gap lengthened.

In Malawi, fertiliser was available to farmers at government-subsidised prices until the 1980s, when the country was forced to devalue its currency several times and prices of imported fertilisers quadrupled as a result. The World

Bank recognised that greater use of fertilisers was essential to increase agricultural productivity in Malawi, but at the same time it argued that the government could not afford to continue to subsidise fertiliser. After a protracted struggle lasting eight years, the Fertiliser Subsidy Removal Programme was completed in 1995, signalling a temporary victory for the Bank. However, concern about the consequences for food security and hunger prompted other donors (led by the UK) to finance the free distribution of fertiliser and improved seed to all farmers in Malawi, through the 'Starter Pack' programme. The impact of Starter Packs was dramatic: the national maize harvest increased by 16 per cent, the hunger season was reduced by one to two months and maize prices were stabilised across seasons. But after bumper harvests in the late 1990s, the Starter Pack programme was scaled down from universal availability to covering just one-third of farmers in the country, which had an immediate negative effect on agricultural productivity and played a role in the 2002 famine.[35]

After another food crisis hit in 2005, the Government of Malawi introduced the Input Subsidy Programme, which again aimed to increase the use of fertilisers and improved varieties of maize seed. The subsidy was delivered to almost half of all farming families nationwide in the form of a voucher that could be redeemed for fertiliser and seeds at one-third of normal retail prices. At first, the donor community disapproved of the programme, for the same reasons that it had lobbied for abolition of fertiliser subsidies in the 1980s, and so the subsidy was financed entirely by government. But the programme was extremely popular and contributed to a bumper harvest in 2006, which prompted the government to renew it with equally positive results in 2007 (although good rainfall, and not the increased use of agricultural inputs alone, played an important role in both years' production totals). After years of decrying the market-inhibiting impacts of input subsidies, international donors now accept that the Input Subsidy Programme in Malawi has a political and popular momentum that is difficult to resist, and are starting to offer technical and financial support.[36]

It should be noted that the past reluctance of rich-country donors to support agricultural subsidies in poor countries reflects a double standard. This is illustrated by our experience of asking a donor official why the United States Agency for International Development (USAID) pushed so hard for the abolition of fertiliser subsidies in Malawi. 'Because subsidies distort the market and undermine private traders,' he explained patiently. 'Then why does the United States government subsidise and protect your own farmers so heavily?' we asked. 'Because we can afford subsidies,' he stated. 'Malawi can't.'

In addition to price subsidies, targeted input vouchers, input trade fairs and inputs-for-work schemes can also help deliver agricultural inputs to farmers. Small-scale inputs-for-work projects have been evaluated favourably in Malawi, both in terms of participant satisfaction and in terms of raising food production.

Financial Services

The lack of access to financial services, particularly affordable credit, is another serious constraint to agricultural productivity and food security. Well-functioning credit markets assist households in making yield-enhancing investments (like irrigation, fertiliser and improved seed) in their farm systems.

In Malawi, the story of credit access is similar to that of fertiliser access. In the 1980s, over 400,000 small farmers in Malawi were members of 'farmers' clubs' organised by the Ministry of Agriculture. They enjoyed access to subsidised credit that allowed them to buy fertiliser and seeds at affordable prices. Farmers stood security for each other, and more than 90 per cent repaid their loans, which assured them of getting credit again the following year. But in 1995 the government-run Smallholder Agricultural Credit Association was converted into the Malawi Rural Finance Corporation, a private company that offers loans on a commercial basis only to wealthier farmers, excluding the poor and food insecure farmers, who are seen as too risky. Now lack of access to subsidised credit pushes many poor families in Malawi to turn to private moneylenders. These moneylenders often charge annual interest rates of 100 per cent or more on the offered loans. Should the harvest fail, these families will find themselves heavily in debt.[37]

However, the future of pro-poor rural microfinance seems to be bright, particularly in Asia. Following on the heels of the widely publicised success of Bangladesh's Grameen Bank – for which its founder Mohammed Yunus won the Nobel Peace Prize in 2006 – a number of 'social entrepreneurs' have started rural microfinance institutions of their own. These organisations have shown that it is possible for the private sector to both run profitable companies and offer loans to poor rural families at very low interest. Approaches such as group lending models, in which loans are granted to a group that collectively takes on the responsibility of ensuring that each individual member pays back their share, have resulted in very low default rates. Following the success of these private organisations, some governments are even getting back into the rural microfinance act; India has started a large-scale scheme wherein the government helps to organise women's groups and then links them to commercial banks that provide small low-interest loans.

*   *   *

The battle against seasonal hunger must be fought on several fronts: emergency assistance to protect lives and assets during the hunger months; social protection safety nets to minimise the number of families who require emergency assistance; and agricultural livelihoods development initiatives to work towards a future when safety nets are rarely needed. As Kates and Millman write, 'not all food shortages lead to hunger; not all hunger leads to starvation; not all starvation causes death'.[38] The chain is broken by good policy, and the measures we discuss above are a key part of a good policy package.

But despite the plethora of proven-effective ideas, seasonal hunger persists. Too few of the ideas above make the journey from paper to the real world of the rural poor, and those that do often work in isolation, like islands of protection amidst an ocean of vulnerability. We argue that this is so primarily because hunger remains low on the list of global political priorities, and as a result anti-hunger efforts do not receive the kind of resources they need to be effective and universal. Put simply, all the good ideas in the world will not be enough to end hunger if laws and money are also not present – laws to ensure that the human right to food becomes legally enforceable, not just an uncertain outcome of the present political environment; and money to finance a universal, integrated intervention framework in all countries at risk of seasonal hunger. We explore these issues in the next chapter.

3
From Policy to Rights

In a country where there is plenty of food, every child, woman and man dying from hunger is assassinated.

A.W. Ray, Chief Justice of the Uttar Pradesh State High Court, India

The Godavari River rises just east of the Arabian Sea and flows across the breadth of central India, finally emptying into the Bay of Bengal after a journey of some 1,500 kilometres. Its terminus, in the districts of West and East Godavari of Andhra Pradesh state, is one of India's most fertile rice-growing areas. Distinct seasons do indeed pass by here – the monsoon months, the dry winter, and the rainless yet stiflingly humid summer – but the land stays evergreen, fed by a web of streamlets and irrigation canals.

Subhalakshmi farms a single hectare in the river delta of West Godavari. She and her two adult sons grow some of the dozens of varieties of chilli peppers for which the state of Andhra Pradesh is so famous. Despite the geographical good fortune that provides her with year-round irrigation, the seasons still matter for Subhalakshmi. The lion's share of her income comes at one time of the year, during the chilli harvest. At planting time, she borrows heavily from local private moneylenders to finance the year's farm operations, and she depends on the harvest to pay back these debts.

Figure 3.1　One of Subhalakshmi's workers, in West Godavari District, Andhra Pradesh, India.

Things will be hard this year. Early torrential rains – too much water instead of too little – have pounded the chilli crop just at harvest time. Unpicked peppers are beginning to rot on the plants, and those arranged in drying piles on the ground have started to mould. The quality of the peppers is now so poor that the middlemen have cut the buying price by half in just the last few days. The price crash, combined with the drop in overall sellable production, has reduced the income of chilli farmers like Subhalakshmi by as much as three-quarters this year. Unless she sells the land itself – a decision that would consign her and her sons to future years of deep poverty – she will not be able to repay her debt.

'If people like you,' Subhalakshmi says to us sharply when our team of researchers stop by her field to talk, 'don't have mercy on us this year, we are finished.' By 'people like

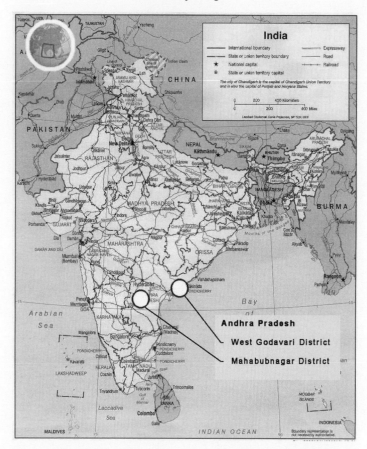

Figure 3.2 West Godavari and Mahabubnagar Districts
in the state of Andhra Pradesh, India.

Source: University of Texas Libraries.

you' she means specifically the moneylenders, although our
clothes and our car are enough to lump us all in the same
category: non-seasonal people, perhaps. At first she sees some
hope in us coming to talk to her; in response to last year's
widespread crop failures, the Indian government had just

the previous week granted a massive loan waiver to farmers across the country.[1] But the waiver applies only to farmers who took loans from commercial banks, not from private moneylenders, as Subhalakshmi and other poor farmers did. She asks if we are from the government, perhaps with hopes of the waiver in mind, and we tell her that we are not: we are here only to ask questions. She sighs in impatience, but talks to us nevertheless.

Figure 3.3   Subhalakshmi, talking to us in her field, West Godavari District, Andhra Pradesh, India.

Copyright © E. Whelan.

It is not long before the conversation turns from this year's poor harvest to the larger drama of agrarian distress in the country. Over the last decade, an astonishing wave of farmer suicides has swept across India. Across the country, some 160,000 farmers – almost one every half an hour – have killed themselves, and the state of Andhra Pradesh is one of the epicentres of the tragedy.[2] The suicide crisis illustrates with distressing clarity the extreme fragility of the economic situation in which many of India's small farmers find themselves, a fragility linked closely to cycles of crop failure and insurmountable debt. Subhalakshmi refers to this ongoing crisis when she tells us angrily that 'there are times when suicide seems like the only option'.

Subhalakshmi's poor harvest will affect many more families than just her own. She typically hires a dozen or so people to work as day labourers during the harvest. It is not the most irreproachable of labour arrangements – some of those hired are children who should be going to school, others are elderly and struggle to do the work, and the wages are meagre – but in any case the harvest is a critical income-earning time for these poor families; during other months of the year, work is scarce. With the damage the rains have inflicted on her chilli crop, however, Subhalakshmi will have to cut back on her labour force during this year's harvest.

HOLES IN THE NET

Subhalakshmi's problems are not difficult to identify: she does not have agricultural insurance; she does not benefit from a guaranteed floor price for her chilli peppers; and she has little access to other employment that could supplement her farm income in bad years like this one. Although she lives in India, a country that on paper has one of the most impressive anti-hunger intervention frameworks in the world – including many of the ideas we mentioned in the previous chapter – she finds herself falling through the large holes in the social protection safety net. In the first half of this chapter, we look at this safety net in India, profiling its commendable successes while examining the holes that exist and how they may be mended.

Overall, despite the country's much-vaunted recent rapid economic growth and the presence of the safety net, hunger and malnutrition are still rampant in India, even higher than in most Sub-Saharan countries. At least 200 million adults in the country suffer from seasonal energy stress.[3] Nearly 20 per cent of preschool children in the country suffer from acute malnutrition.[4] This latter figure is one of the highest rates in the world. In fact, the World Health Organisation considers a 15 per cent acute malnutrition rate to be the emergency threshold, even in humanitarian crises; by this standard, India as a whole is in a state of constant nutritional emergency, year in and year out. At least two states, Madhya Pradesh and Jharkhand, have acute malnutrition rates exceeding *twice* that threshold, a truly catastrophic situation.

*   *   *

Despite all of her problems, Subhalakshmi is in the fortunate minority of Indian farmers who have access to irrigation. Nearly 70 per cent of India's agricultural lands are classified as 'rainfed' and depend solely on the four to five month mid-year monsoon period.[5] Over much of these lands, only one crop a year can be grown, resulting in a highly seasonal income pattern for farmers. During the dry season, many farmers join the ranks of the permanently landless in seeking wage labour work off their farms.

The people of Annapanenivari Gudem live only 40 kilometres to the west of Subhalakshmi, but the distance is far enough that the delta irrigation systems do not reach

Figure 3.4 Farmer and his fields in the dry season, Annapanenivari Gudem, Andhra Pradesh, India.

the village. The farms are fed by rain only, and outside the monsoon months, the land is dry and cracked, resembling less the stereotypical image of the fertile, green Godavari delta than the aridity of India's north-central plains. We talk to families in Annapanenivari Gudem during the height of the dry season, and their replies to our questions are punctuated by gestures to the fallow hectares that lie around them. 'We have the land to grow food,' is the oft-repeated lament, 'but there is no water.'

Figure 3.5   The people of Annapanenivari Gudem, working as day labourers in nearby fields.

Copyright © E. Whelan.

In decades past, the irrigated delta areas in West Godavari were simply too far away from Annapanenivari Gudem for the villagers to migrate daily in search of work, and their only income came from selling their own single annual harvest. But in recent years, rural infrastructure has improved – good roads built, labour information networks broadened – and now farmers from the delta send trucks daily to Annapaneni-vari Gudem to pick up willing labourers in the early morning and drop them back home in the evening. Yet despite the improved job opportunities, nearly half of the year's wages are still concentrated in the early monsoon months of June through August, as Figure 3.6 shows.[6] During the low-work months, especially the immediate pre-monsoon period of March through May when last year's saved income has dwindled, the families of Annapanenivari Gudem constrict their daily meals to rice, *dhal*,[7] and sometimes a simple curry. Vegetables, fruit, milk and eggs – much less meat of any kind – are never eaten in this period. The diet is far from adequate: seasonal hunger persists.

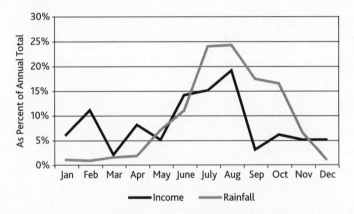

Figure 3.6   Seasonal cycles of income and rainfall in Annapanenivari Gudem.

Source: Rainfall data from Department of Agriculture, West Godavari district.
Income data from participatory exercise conducted by the authors.

But the picture in Annapanenivari Gudem is yet more complex. Figure 3.7 shows the monthly percentages of underweight preschoolers over the harvest-to-harvest period between September 2006 and August 2007. The top line is the percentage of preschool children who are mildly, moderately, or severely underweight; the middle line is the percentage of moderately or severely underweight only; and the bottom line is the percentage of severely underweight only. The patterns for all three are strikingly flat – they are non-seasonal. Yet the overall percentages for each remain alarmingly high.

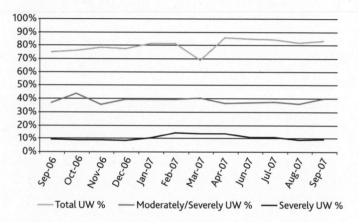

Figure 3.7   Seasonal pattern of malnutrition in Annapanenivari Gudem.

Source: Anganwadi centre, Annapanenivari Gudem.

So what is happening in Annapanenivari Gudem? What prevents seasonal patterns of rainfall and income from leading to a spike in child underweight rates – as occurs in Malawi and other countries – but does not significantly reduce the total underweight percentage nor address the annual lean season contraction in dietary diversity? The answers likely have to do with the successes and shortcomings of the social protection mechanisms that exist in the village (and universally in India), particularly the Public Distribution System (PDS) and the Integrated Child Development Services (ICDS) scheme.

The Public Distribution System

India is the largest provider of food assistance in the world, and the vehicle for this assistance is the Public Distribution System. The PDS buys grains and other staple foods from farmers across the country and sells them back to poor families at heavily subsidised prices; for the poorest of the poor, the current price in Annapanenivari Gudem and other villages in Andhra Pradesh is around 2 rupees (about 3p) per kilogram.[8] The price is held constant regardless of season.

The PDS has its roots in the years just before India's independence, particularly in the aftermath of the disastrous Bengal famine of 1943. The famine claimed at least 2 million lives,[9] not due to a shortage of grain in the country, but rather because poor families could not afford food prices driven sharply upward by a combination of an inflationary wartime economy, speculative grain hoarding, and hunger season income and price trends.[10] A way to prevent such future catastrophic events was clearly needed. Following independence in 1947, a network of 'fair price shops' began to be created across the country, private-run but government-supplied outlets for subsidised sales of grains and staple foods to the public. As the decades passed, the public distribution system was further institutionalised and expanded until it became an integral part – arguably the core – of the government's anti-hunger policy. In 2004/05, the total cost to the Indian government of running the system was well in excess of £3 billion, or around 1 per cent of the country's Gross Domestic Product.[11] Nearly half a million fair price shops are currently in operation across India, including one in Annapanenivari Gudem.

But with expansion of the PDS came mounting costs and 'leakage' of food to corrupt bureaucrats, non-poor families, and middlemen involved in procurement, transport, storage and sales. In response, the system was changed in 1997 to a 'targeted' approach, wherein only families identified as having incomes below the poverty line ('pink card' families) were offered the heavily subsidised selling price.[12] Above the poverty line 'white card' families were sold the grain at cost.

The policy change proved to be controversial, and of questionable effectiveness. Accurately distinguishing poor from non-poor families is difficult in any country, but in India, where that distinction has to be made for several hundred million families, the task is enormous – and further complicated by the fact that the official Indian poverty line is in the eyes of many analysts extremely low, leading to underestimates of the true extent of poverty.[13] Exclusion of many poor families was inevitable: a government-commissioned evaluation of the targeted PDS concluded in 2001 that less than three in five poor households were actually reached by the scheme. The leakage problems also persisted; only 42 per cent of all of the food in the programme actually reached the poor, the rest lost to corruption and incorrect provision to non-poor families.[14] In addition, the food subsidy extends only to staple foods but not to fruits, vegetables and other key components of a diverse diet, thus improving the quantity of food accessed by the poor but not necessarily the quality. The final irony is that the costs for the targeted PDS proved to be even higher than for the earlier programme. This is largely because the failures of targeting led to fewer families accessing the mountains of procured food grains stored in the government granaries; as a result, storage costs skyrocketed.

Forty per cent is better than none at all, however, and it is worth observing that even attempting to run a system of near-universal provision of cheap basic foods to hundreds of millions of families, extending almost uninterrupted over six decades, is an impressive signal that hunger is a central concern of the Indian state. The families in Annapanenivari Gudem noted the value of the PDS in improving their ability to access staple grains in the lean season, and this consistent access contributes to keeping child underweight rates stable throughout the year. But in our conversations, compliments for the PDS were more often than not followed in the next breath by justified complaints about poor targeting, leakage, and other problems for which there is little political accountability. The gap between what the Public Distribution System is and what it could be is large: while the households of Annapanenivari Gudem benefit from cheap PDS prices, both the quantity and quality of the food made available are insufficient to prevent high overall underweight rates and lean season contractions of dietary diversity.

Integrated Child Development Services

As with many of India's social protection initiatives, the Integrated Child Development Services (ICDS) scheme – a growth promotion initiative of the type we discussed in the previous chapter – is the largest of its kind in the world. Its services are targeted at all pregnant and lactating women, preschool children and adolescent girls in India, and include antenatal and postnatal care, growth monitoring, immunisation, micronutrient supplementation, health and nutrition education, supplementary feeding, and preschool education. ICDS' delivery is admirably decentralised, relying on a network of 'Anganwadi centres', multi-purpose facilities set up in each village to serve as the simultaneous delivery point for all of the services. The staff of each centre consists at a minimum of one female Anganwadi worker-supervisor and one assistant *ayah* responsible for watching the children during the day-care hours. The staff members are usually residents of the community in which the centre is located.

The Anganwadi centre in Annapanenivari Gudem is small but brightly decorated. Health and nutrition posters mingle with the children's drawings on the walls; colourful photos hang on the lengths of twine strung across the low rafters. Even in the height of the dry season, the garden is kept beautifully lush and filled with flowers, a small well serving as the year-round watering source. Behind the garden is an ample playground.

The first time we visit the centre, the Anganwadi worker is away, so we spend the afternoon chatting to the *ayah*, Kumari. Around eight-thirty every morning, the mothers and grandmothers of the village leave their small children, about 30 in all, with Kumari. The *ayah* supervises their play and leads them through some preschool learning activities until the morning meal, around eleven o'clock. The meal is small and simple, usually a helping of rice and *dhal*, with some vegetables if available. The children take short naps after lunch and go home by one or two o'clock.

It is clear from our conversations with Kumari – and in later days with the Anganwadi worker, a young woman named Siromani – that the ICDS services have, since their inception three decades ago, become an indispensable part of life in the community. It is also clear that, despite the calm professionalism with which the women carry out their duties, they

Figure 3.8   Kumari, the ayah at the Anganwadi centre
in Annapanenivari Gudem.

are severely overburdened. The combination of health and nutrition extension, growth monitoring, feeding, preschool supervision, and other activities is simply too much for two people to handle effectively, and the quality of the services provided suffers as a result. Besides the shortage of staff, other major issues include a lack of adequate equipment, nearly non-existent supervision and training, and a serious shortfall in the resources required to provide the quantity and quality of food needed by the mothers and children. The basic underlying issue is that the ICDS design did not consider deeply enough how to embed systems of account-ability – systems that would have forced policymakers to notice the staff and resource shortages years ago, and respond accordingly – that are critical to bridge the gap between good ideas and successful implementation.

The result is that the ICDS interventions in Annapanenivari Gudem are having less of an impact than they could. The largest problem appears to be in addressing the nutritional needs of pregnant and lactating mothers. An analysis of panel data from all 54 children attending from the Anganwadi centre shows the underweight percentage does in fact decline considerably between the ages of one and five, indicating that the ICDS services to preschool children are having an impact (although worryingly high underweight rates remain among all groups, as Figure 3.7 above implies). Extremely high underweight rates, however, persist from birth to about nine months, indicating that services are less effectively reaching pregnant and lactating women.

There are, however, many reasons for hope. While some technical improvements could certainly be made, ICDS' intervention strategy is strikingly sound, even innovative in its attempts to address the food, care and health determinants of malnutrition in a holistic manner. Though three decades have passed since ICDS was first rolled out, even today few programmes anywhere in the world adopt this essential multi-sectoral approach to child nutrition.

Spending time with the Anganwadi children also certainly increases one's optimism about the ICDS programme. Bhumika is a cheerful three-year-old who, in between giggles, talks with us at the Anganwadi centre. Despite her giggles, the little girl is improbably polite: she finishes every sentence with the word '*undi*', which in the local language Telugu means 'madam' or 'sir' – an oddly formal expression for such a small child, even here in rural India. But the politeness is part of a larger clear-headedness about her; when we ask what she wants to do when she gets older, she gestures at the Anganwadi centre and says, 'I'm going to the little school now. I want to go to the big school when I grow up.' In a country where many

Figure 3.9   Bhumika, at the Anganwadi centre.

girls marry as young teenagers, and some never go to school at all, it is moving to hear a three-year-old speak about her hope for education. The credit must be given to Kumari and Siromani, and to ICDS in general.

*   *   *

In addition to the PDS and ICDS, other social protection measures are active in Annapanenivari Gudem, including crop support prices, pensions and micro-loans.

At the beginning of each agricultural cycle, a government body called the Commission on Agricultural Costs and Prices uses estimates of production costs to recommend 'minimum support prices' – floor prices – for a wide variety of crops. These are the rates at which the central government guarantees that it will buy the crops come harvest time, should prevailing market prices be very low. The minimum support prices protect farmers against the adverse seasonal price volatility that we saw in Malawi and other countries.[15] There are, however, holes in the minimum support system; procurement of the harvest does not occur in some remote areas,[16] and certain crops are left out, like Subhalakshmi's chilli peppers.

Social pensions and insurance schemes, both run by the government, are also active in Annapanenivari Gudem. Pensions of £2.50/month are provided to the most vulnerable groups in the village: the elderly and infirm, widows, the disabled and the lowest castes. The insurance scheme requires a premium payment of about £1.65 a year and provides coverage for severe illness, disability and death.[17]

Additionally, government-facilitated subsidised loans flow from banks to women's financial cooperatives in the village. These 'self-help groups' manage the loans collectively, granting portions to each member for small business ventures while adding to their total portfolio through the savings of each household. Group vigilance over individual loan payback ensures that the default rate is kept very low. The loans themselves are often very small, but effective. Kumari's self-help group of ten women, for example, borrowed about £500 from a local bank. With her £50 share, Kumari bought a buffalo. She sells milk from the buffalo to a government dairy, and makes enough net profit to buy a little extra food a month for her family, while paying back about £2.50 a month to the bank.

* * *

To return to our original question: what is happening in Annapanenivari Gudem to cause seasonality of underweight prevalence among preschool children to be muted, but not seasonality of dietary diversity nor high rates of malnutrition in general? Our look at social protection programmes suggests that they – in combination with the increased economic opportunities allowing access to work in irrigated areas – are indeed effective to an extent. The PDS ensures that families can purchase from fair price shops year-round at a low, constant price; storage of food is thus not a key concern. The ICDS provides supplementary meals, and is having a moderate impact on reducing malnutrition among children between the ages of one and five. Pensions, insurance and micro-loans provide further income opportunities and safety nets. All these social protection measures together probably explain why underweight rates are relatively constant throughout the year.

Yet there are serious holes in the safety net, which relate not to a lack of 'good ideas' but rather to poor and limited implementation. More than half the food meant to go to the poor is lost in the PDS system. Nationwide, the PDS meets only 10–30 per cent of the individual food needs of those who do access the system,[18] and there is little diversity of food available beyond basic grains and staples. The food offered by ICDS is limited to one meal a day, and again restricted in diversity. Work overload prevents the Anganwadi staff from performing their duties to the best of their ability; services to pregnant and lactating women stand out in their lack of observed impact. Wage-earning opportunities have indeed increased in recent years, but jobs are still scarce and incomes low for much of the year. The persistence of these problems leads to the present situation: a continuing lean season when little more than rice and *dhal* is consumed, as well as an overall high underweight rate among preschool children.

THE POWER OF LAW

As we detailed in the previous section, many of the ideas we argued for in Chapter 2 are in place in India, from subsidised staple foods to growth promotion programmes to crop support prices. But it is clear that all these good ideas are not good enough; seasonal diet restrictions and malnutrition persist in villages like Annapanenivari Gudem because the programmes are not working as well as they should. When we examine why, we return again and again to the reality that the full potential of these programmes is constrained by political factors: apathetic implementation, bureaucratic obstructionism and outright corruption. The issue, fundamentally, is one of power imbalance. When policy, no matter how enlightened, is not supported by mechanisms by which the poor can demand effective, honest implementation, its success becomes dependent on the commitment of policymakers – a commitment that history has shown to be fickle and half-hearted at best, even in a functioning democracy like India's.

But how to fight political apathy, bureaucracy and corruption? Even to ask such an impossibly large question invites frustrated sighs and hopeless shrugs; but India itself provides answers and inspiration. Over the past decade, a coalition of citizens and civil society organisations has launched the Right to Food Campaign (RTFC), a movement to end hunger in India. The RTFC is both pragmatic and tremendously ambitious in its goals: pragmatic in that it does not demand a radical transformation in the policy environment, yet ambitious in its struggle to ensure that the policies that are supposed to already be in place – the Public Distribution System and Integrated Child Development Services among them – are implemented according to the full letter of their intent. And even further: that these policies should become legal entitlements, not subject to the undependable commitment of policymakers and implementers.

The movement started with a lawsuit. In 2001, severe drought hit India's northwest state of Rajasthan, resulting in numerous deaths from starvation and malnutrition. Meanwhile, partly because the new 'targeted' approach of the Public Distribution System prevented millions of families from buying subsidised food, the central government's grain reserves reached massive proportions, exceeding 50 million metric tonnes by 2002. The grotesque incongruity between death by starvation and mountainous food stocks

---

Box 3.1 Founding Statement of the Right to Food Campaign

'The right to food campaign is an informal network of organisations and individuals committed to the realisation of the right to food in India. We consider that everyone has a fundamental right to be free from hunger and undernutrition. Realising this right requires not only equitable and sustainable food systems, but also entitlements relating to livelihood security such as the right to work, land reform and social security. We consider that the primary responsibility for guaranteeing these entitlements rests with the state. Lack of financial resources cannot be accepted as an excuse for abdicating this responsibility. In the present context, where people's basic needs are not a political priority, state intervention itself depends on effective popular organisation. We are committed to fostering this process through all democratic means.'

---

led to a civil society organisation called the People's Union for Civil Liberties (PUCL) to file public interest litigation with India's Supreme Court, alleging that the government had a legal obligation to use the stocks to feed the hungry. The lawsuit specifically references Article 21 of the Indian Constitution, which states that protecting 'the right to life', and by implication the right to food, is a fundamental responsibility of the state.[19]

The lawsuit continues to this day – the final judgement may not arrive for years yet – but in the intervening years, the focus of the litigation has greatly broadened. A network of organisations joined the PUCL in founding the Right to Food Campaign to coordinate public activism around the legal effort, and today the 'right to food case', as it is popularly known, is not simply a challenge to starvation deaths in Rajasthan alone, but rather to the presence of any kind of hunger in any part of India.

And there have been major victories. The Supreme Court, though still deliberating on the litigation itself, has issued a series of strongly worded 'Interim Orders' which direct the government to immediately expand and improve the existing social protection programmes. Specific instructions have been issued to increase the coverage of the PDS and the ICDS and other anti-hunger programmes; but the greatest force of the Supreme Court judgement comes in the delineation of clear lines of accountability throughout the political structure. Specially appointed Commissioners monitor whether political and administrative authorities are in compliance with the Interim Orders, and have a further responsibility to hear and respond to grievances from citizens. A very strong Right to Information Act passed in 2005, as well as a system of 'social audits' promoted by the RTFC, further increase the ability of citizens to monitor and evaluate government response to these orders. In effect, the Supreme Court has transformed social protection policy into legal entitlement and attempted to enforce a framework for transparency around this entitlement.

The greatest achievement of the Right to Food Campaign thus far, however, may be its success in pushing for a universal 'right to work' – which is, for the majority of poor families, the most important legal entitlement that could be provided in the fight against seasonal hunger. In August 2005, after years of activism by the RTFC, India's Parliament passed the National Rural Employment Guarantee Act (NREGA), which guarantees every rural household the legal right to be provided with public sector work for 100 days a year at the minimum wage. Households are entitled to an unemployment allowance if the government is unable to provide work within two weeks of a request for employment.

The Act is a slightly diluted version of what the RTFC was originally pushing for – the campaign wanted an employment guarantee that was neither limited to rural areas nor to a 100 days per year ceiling – but the NREGA is still one of the strongest anti-hunger legislations ever enacted, in any country. Implementation of the Act, which began in the form of the National Rural Employment Guarantee Scheme (NREGS) in February 2006, has had its bumps: the informational and administrative requirements are massive, and governmental structures are adapting very slowly to NREGS' needs; systems of patronage and corruption that have survived, even thrived from, past development programmes are strongly resistant to the transparency demanded by NREGS; and poor families themselves, after six decades (and centuries more) of being treated, at best, as 'beneficiaries' and not as 'rights-holders', will take time to adjust to and fully exercise their new legal entitlements. Largely as a result of these issues, evaluations of NREGS from across the country show mixed results in its first two years of implementation, with wide variations in performance between states and districts. The second year of its existence, however, was markedly improved over the first, and the concerted watchdog efforts of the Right to Food Campaign are having an impact on holding NREGS to its course. The future looks bright.

And if you ask the people of villages like Jaklair, a small community we visited in the drought-prone western areas of Andhra Pradesh, they will tell you that NREGS has been a godsend. In the past, getting one's name on the beneficiary list for government employment programmes was a question of begging or paying the right authorities. Now, most share the sentiments of Lingamma, a quiet woman in her mid twenties, who tells us that she would 'be daring enough to demand any of [the village officials] for work' under NREGS. With improved transparency in record-keeping and a system that avoids contractors and other middlemen, payment of salaries is more honest and consistent. Delays in salary payments still occur, but the NREGS workers of Jaklair laughingly attribute that to a slow postmaster rather than corruption. There is an assurance in their voices that the payment may come late, but it will come – a departure from the past when the cheques could have been lost in the pockets of any of a host of intermediaries.

Despite our prodding, the villagers report no major problems with the NREGS other than the late pay-cheques – in stark contrast to their withering criticism of other ongoing social protection programmes. The Public Distribution System's targeting exercise has been extremely flawed in Jaklair: many families living well below the poverty line do not have the coveted 'pink card' that entitles them to subsidised prices, and constant complaints to the government have yielded no result. Despite the clear commitment of their staff, none of the three Anganwadi centres in the village have had working child-growth scales for the last two years, again despite repeated requests to the ICDS authorities. The Anganwadi women do the best they can, but being unable to monitor the weight and growth of the village children, a core function of their work is undermined.

The difference between these two programmes and NREGS is that the concept of legal entitlement has been embedded in the latter since its inception. While the Interim Orders covering ICDS and PDS transform the benefits of these programmes as well into legal entitlements, implementation of these orders has reached neither Jaklair nor most of India's villages. If the Right to Food Campaign continues its work, however, that may soon change. The Interim Orders, as powerful as they are in spirit, need activism to be made real; as the Campaign itself puts it, 'the implementation of Supreme Court orders depends crucially on organised public demand. Without public pressure, the orders typically remain on paper. The orders are just a helpful "stick" to keep the government on its toes. But hands are needed to lift the stick and use it.'[20]

One can imagine a PDS and ICDS that operate along the same rights-based lines as NREGS. In practice, this would likely mean a return to the untargeted PDS, which allows any citizen, regardless of any questionable external calculation of their socio-economic status, to claim their right to an affordable diet. For ICDS, this will mean that every pregnant and lactating mother, adolescent girl and preschool child has a legal entitlement to demand a set of nutritional and health services. The extent of the entitlement might expand depending on nutritional status; children identified as severely malnourished might automatically be entitled to therapeutic treatment, for example.[21]

NREGS has not solved every problem in Jaklair. As Figure 3.10 shows, seasonal constrictions of diet are still common. As in Annapanenivari Gudem, a wide range of social protection programmes need to be improved if a genuine food security is to be achieved in Jaklair; NREGS alone will not be enough. But we can clearly see in Jaklair a nascent process of empowerment that is transferring control over development processes from the political and administrative structure to the electorate. Through NREGS, the governed make demands of the government: a truly revolutionary change from the optional beneficence of past anti-hunger programmes.

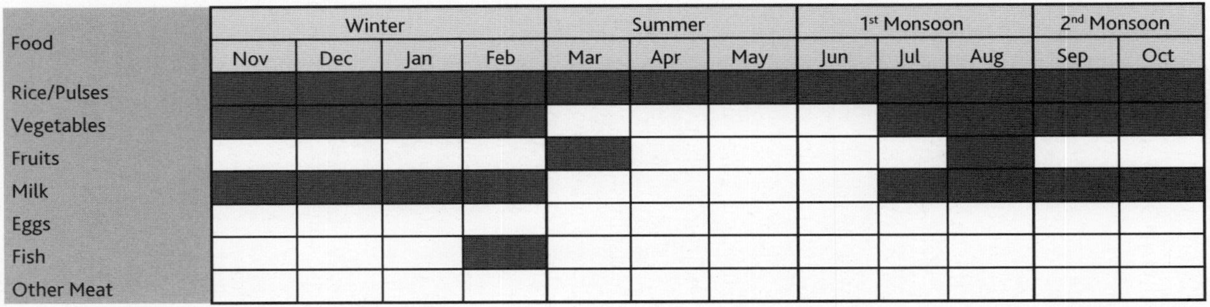

Food	Winter				Summer			1st Monsoon			2nd Monsoon	
	Nov	Dec	Jan	Feb	Mar	Apr	May	Jun	Jul	Aug	Sep	Oct
Rice/Pulses	■	■	■	■	■	■	■	■	■	■	■	■
Vegetables	■	■	■	■	■	■	■	■	■	■	■	■
Fruits				■	■				■	■	■	
Milk	■	■	■	■				■	■	■		■
Eggs				■								
Fish												
Other Meat												

Figure 3.10 Seasonal dietary diversity in Jaklair, Andhra Pradesh, India. Boxes are shaded if families eat the indicated food group at least three times a week. From group discussion conducted by authors.

THE MOVEMENT FORWARD:
AN INTERNATIONAL RIGHT TO FOOD

The implementation of programmes – no matter how technically well-conceived – will fall apart without a fundamental transformation in the political obligations around hunger. It is the struggle for this transformation that we are witnessing in India today. The Right to Food Campaign teaches us that there is no need to wait for enlightened leadership; citizens worldwide can demand that the right to food be made legally enforceable.

So, to confront the question head-on: how do we build on successes like those in India to create a system for genuine protection of the right to food, both at the international and national levels? Several useful legal instruments around the right to food already exist in the international treaty structure, particularly the International Covenant on Economic, Social and Cultural Rights (ICESCR) and the Convention on the Rights of the Child (CRC). While these treaties deal with a broad set of entitlements, articles within each specifically address the right of human beings to be free from hunger.[22] The vast majority of nations – 145 in the case of the ICESCR and 192 in the case of the CRC[23] – have ratified these treaties, implying a commitment on the part of the signatory governments to regard the contents of the ICESCR and the CRC as legally binding.

In principle, these global agreements have several important functions. Their primary objective, as presently understood, is to guide the incorporation of rights into national law. In some countries – Norway is a notably strong example – international treaties are 'self-executing', which means that they automatically take on the force of law in domestic courts.

In most countries, however, specific national legislation needs to be passed to affirm the applicability of international law in the domestic arena. Thus far, about 20 countries in the world have included the right to food (or very closely related rights, such as the right to life) in their national constitutions, an action which lays a foundation for future 'justicability' – the ability of the judicial system to rule on alleged violations of the right to food. It was such a constitutional article on the right to life that India's Supreme Court used to defend its Interim Orders converting anti-hunger programmes into legal entitlements. Rulings like these are beginning to set legal precedents that will be very useful in how the right to food should be interpreted and adjudicated in other countries.

The best-case scenario, however, is for national legal systems to go beyond relying on judicial interpretation of constitutional rights. Instead, national framework legislation that specifies what exactly the right to food legally means in each country – how violation is defined, what enforcement procedures for remedy are appropriate, and so on – would be valuable. We suggest that the social protection safety net described in the previous chapter could inform a definition of what the right to food specifically means: legally entitled access to employment, pensions, community growth promotion programmes and so on. If the state fails to fulfil those particular entitlements, citizens would have the right to demand remedy through the judicial system.

The purpose of strong global agreements such as the ICESCR and the CRC goes beyond simply guiding national right to food legislation, however. It is reasonable to assume that even in the presence of national legislation there will be instances where governments fail to safeguard their citizens' right to food. As with violations of civil and political rights, such as genocide and torture, the international community will need to be able to exercise legal force in compelling states to comply with the right to food. Unfortunately, at present there are few strong international judicial mechanisms to enforce the right to food; these need to be created.

The first step would be to strengthen the Committee on Economic, Social and Cultural Rights (CESCR), a United Nations-affiliated body that oversees the progress of signatory nations towards fulfilment of the ICESCR. While the body has been valuable in helping to specify the meaning of the right to food and states' obligations under the ICESCR, it has no procedure for receiving complaints of rights violations from individuals or groups; at present, only governments or NGOs can file reports on violations. An 'Optional Protocol' to the ICESCR has recently been drafted that would remedy this situation by creating a complaints structure around the Committee, similar to the one that already exists under an international sister treaty defining civil and political rights. Finalising this Protocol would be an immediate way to increase the meaningfulness of the ICESCR across borders.

Ultimately, however, the right of food needs real, strong international justicability, not just a complaints mechanism. As Warren Allemand, the president of Rights and Democracy, a Canadian NGO, says: 'We live in a world where it is more serious to break trade rules than it is to violate human rights.'[24] The only way this situation can be changed is to eventually grant jurisdiction over the right to food to judicial mechanisms like the International Court of Justice (ICJ) and the International Criminal Court (ICC), much as the international community is progressively granting jurisdiction over trade matters to the World Trade Organisation. Speaking in 'rights language' has of late become the fashion in governments and NGOs alike, but commitment to rights implies far more than an ethical stance: it implies a willingness to exist within structures of accountability. It is true that developing a consensus among nearly 200 countries on the exact letter of this accountability will be a long and difficult process, but the 'Voluntary Guidelines on the Right to Food' drafted by the UN Food and Agriculture Organisation a few years ago are a good start. Narrower statutes, perhaps based on the package of seasonal hunger-focused social protection measures suggested earlier, could be drawn from the Voluntary Guidelines as a foundation for international right to food law.[25]

An international right to food structure might also work with signatories to develop national 'Zero Hunger' plans, thus not only requiring adherence to law, but also supporting countries in a constructive process of anti-hunger planning. Zero Hunger plans could concentrate on four components: 1) a *financing strategy* that combines existing national and international commitments with additional needs requested from the international donor community; 2) a *technical strategy* for achieving measurable impact on hunger and malnutrition while embedding rights mechanisms in the proposed technical approaches; 3) a *capacity-building strategy* for ensuring that impact can be sustained indefinitely by the relevant public sector agencies; and 4) an *accountability* strategy for reducing corruption and resource leakage, while providing citizen-accessible programme transparency.

The obvious political obstacle is that many governments will see an international right to food structure as a threat to national sovereignty. This is where home-grown movements like India's Right to Food Campaign will be key players in increasing domestic public pressure on governments to accept accountability for guaranteeing the right to food. Ultimately, the choice to internationalise protection of the right to food belongs to each national populace, and the effort to mobilise public opinion in this direction will have to be led by an energised and committed local civil society movement.

THE COST OF ENDING SEASONAL HUNGER

A child may have the misfortune of being born in a poor country, but that child is not born in a poor world.
George Kent, 'Freedom from Want'

Globalising accountability for the right to food implies obligations not just for poor countries, but also for wealthier countries, particularly in providing the resources to make the eradication of hunger a realistic goal. As the Voluntary Guidelines and the ICESCR acknowledge, poor nations can be expected to only 'progressively' advance towards the ideal of a society free from hunger and malnutrition.[26] Given resource constraints, this caveat of progressive realisation is only fair – but ultimately has the effect of diluting the expectations of the right to food agreements, as well as being inappropriate in the face of the severe physical, intellectual and emotional consequences hunger and malnutrition inflicts on people every day, especially children. Tying participation in a right to food jurisdiction structure to increased availability of resources, however, would enable governments to speed up the process of realisation, while simultaneously exposing them to stronger accountability for the implementation process.

So what would the universalisation of an anti-seasonal hunger intervention framework cost? The first step is to consider what set of interventions would be at the core of such a framework and should be prioritised. We argue that the first step is to create a strong social protection safety net. Economic growth and private actors may one day be able to effectively fulfil at least some of the roles of social protection, such as employment and pensions. But until that time, the gaps in the economy – and particularly the widening of these gaps that occurs yearly during the hunger season – must be patched by an intervention agenda. In addition, effective social protection can itself fuel economic growth by bolstering human and physical capital.

We suggest that the following programmes, the first of which is emergency-focused and the other three part of a social protection safety net, should comprise a 'minimum essential package':

1. Community-based management of acute malnutrition
2. Employment guarantee programmes
3. Social pensions
4. Child growth promotion

A wide variety of other interventions will certainly be required to fight seasonal hunger effectively, but these four provide a good foundation for action, covering emergency treatment of preschool children and cash/food benefits for households, the elderly, and mothers and children.[27] In addition, although these interventions have the primary objective of fighting seasonal hunger, the positive impacts of each will clearly extend further: they will support year-round household food security, maternal and child health, purchase of essential non-food items, and so on.

The Appendix calculates the rough estimated cost of universalising each of the interventions above. Using those estimates, Figure 3.11 summarises the total cost of our minimum essential package: between £25.81 and £48.52 billion annually, with a mean of £37.17 billion; the Employment Guarantee and pensions comprise the vast majority of this expense.[28]

Intervention	Annual Costs	
	Low Estimate (£ billion)	High Estimate (£ billion)
1. Community-based management of malnutrition	0.96	1.87
2. Employment guarantee schemes	15.00	27.00
3. Social pensions	6.03	12.21
4. Child growth promotion	3.82	7.44
TOTAL	25.81	48.52

Figure 3.11   Estimated cost of anti-seasonal hunger
'minimum essential package'.

The overall cost seems like a great deal of money until one considers that world military spending every year is about half a *trillion* pounds (the total costs of the Iraq war alone will soon exceed that same figure of £500 billion), or enough to fund this package for ten to twenty years. Put another way, if every country in the world were to contribute just 0.1 per cent of its national income – 1/1000th – the collective global total would be nearly £34 billion, which would cover nearly the total cost of the package in the average scenario. This 0.1 per cent figure equates to about 4 pence a day for the average UK resident or 10 cents a day for the average US resident. For this small fraction of income, many of the 36 million people a year who die either directly or indirectly as a result of hunger and malnutrition – including 4 million preschool-age children – would be saved.[29] Achieving the funding target could come through either budgetary increases in donor country food security/nutrition development assistance portfolios or the establishment of a new global pooled fund. The former has the advantage of utilising existing pathways of aid, while the latter would encourage improved global coordination of the fight against hunger.

The ideas above will not be easy to implement, but the fight against hunger demands ambitious strategies. The presence of an international right to food structure is a practical instrument to force countries to confront some important questions: if we have the technical means to end hunger, and if safeguards are in place to ensure against improper use of resources, would rich countries be willing to commit to help finance a new global push to end hunger? And if a commitment to right to food obligations allowed access to the global resources required to fund anti-hunger programmes, would poor countries embark on that commitment? As the right to food scholar George Kent writes, 'If [members of the international community] are serious about sharply reducing the levels of hunger and malnutrition in the world, they should be willing to create a body that would hold them to account for keeping those commitments. They may not be serious. It would be good to challenge them in order to find out if they are.'[30]

* * *

Hunger, and particularly seasonal hunger, may not yet be acknowledged by policymakers as being of fundamental importance. The same, however, is not true for the citizens whom policymakers ostensibly represent. For people from every society, a world free from hunger and malnutrition is the deepest concern; the tremendous outpouring of donations to international NGOs, especially during natural disasters, is clear proof of this. Apart from what is specified in international treaties, it is possible to argue that the right to food has already attained the status of customary law – law that is not necessarily formally codified, but is agreed by all societies to be fundamental and indisputable. Professor of international law Georges Abi-Saab notes that:

> International law, like all law, does not arise from a vacuum or a social void, and does not always emerge in the legal universe in some 'big bang'. In most cases, it is the result of progressive and imperceptible growth, through the process of development of the values of a society; new ideas appear and take root; they strengthen into values which become more and more imperative in the social consciousness, to the point where they give rise to the irresistible conviction that they must be formally approved and protected. That is the point which marks the threshold of law.[31]

If this is true, then perhaps the world is not so far from formalising international right to food law, as well as providing the resources to make that law meaningful. Yet we can hasten the process. Indeed there is lack of political will; but, as Paul Streeten has said, 'It's not political will that we should be studying' – or worrying about – 'but how to create the political base':[32] how to organise effectively to demand of our leaders an increased commitment to fighting hunger across the world. As Box 3.2 shows, there are clear, concrete requests to make: a path to the end of hunger, with signposts along the way.

Box 3.2   The Way Forward for a Universal Right to Food: Key Steps

1. For all remaining states to ratify the International Covenant on Economic, Social and Cultural Rights (ICESCR) and the Convention on the Rights of the Child (CRC).

2. For all states to support the creation of an Optional Protocol for the ICESCR allowing individual and group complaints to be made against violations of the right to food.

3. For all states to adopt constitutional articles explicitly guaranteeing the right to food for their citizens.

4. For all states to create framework legislation around the right to food, specifying legal entitlements of citizens, state obligations and lines of accountability, targets and timetables for reducing hunger and malnutrition, enforcement procedures for remedying violations, and other relevant aspects of defining the right to food in practice.

5. For all states to commit at least 0.1 per cent of their GNP to social protection-centred anti-hunger interventions, along the guidelines of the 'minimum essential package' outlined above, with a particular focus on seasonal hunger. This commitment could come either through larger bilateral food security / nutrition assistance portfolios or a new global fund against hunger.

6. For all states to support the establishment, and accept the authority, of an international judicial structure to prosecute state, group, and individual violations of the right to food.

4
Postscript: Oneness

Just outside the village of Kasiya in central Malawi, tucked on the edge of the final hill before the forest begins, there is a small, beautifully tended field of soybeans. Fourteen farmers from Kasiya own the field collectively – twelve women and two men – but none of them will ever eat or sell these soybeans. Instead, they grow the crop for those in the village who are unable to work: the orphans, disabled and elderly of the village, some 80 people in all. Some of the soybeans will be given directly for cooking, and the rest will be sold to buy food, medicine and clothes.

Other than the soybean seed provided by Action Against Hunger, the rest of the expenses for growing the crop are borne by the farmers. This is not a negligible cost, as the farmers themselves are not wealthy; they too struggle to feed their families in the lean season. Yet even during the height of the hunger months, the time of our visit, we find the women and men working in the field for at least a couple of hours each day, weeding and watering. One look at the field makes it clear that the crop has received this kind of attention since planting. The soybean plants are the largest and healthiest in the village.

The farmers call the project '*Umodze*' – translated into English, 'oneness'.

* * *

In some ways, the messages of this book are 'embarrassingly obvious', as Robert Chambers once wrote about the links between seasonality and poverty.[1] Every year, in the months before the harvest, hundreds of millions of people go hungry. Isolated interventions will never end that cycle; systematic thinking is needed to organise proven effective ideas into a coherent anti-hunger strategy. Solutions must be adapted to local circumstances by the clients. Mechanisms by which people can demand their rights, and the structures to enforce those rights, must be built around all of this. The rich of the world, those with warm hands, must be prepared to provide the lion's share of the funding to make this strategy work.

Yet, as obvious as the answers might be, it will take the tireless, courageous work of a lot of people to make them real – the kind of work that the people of the Umodze project do even in the hunger season, the kind of work that the people of India's Right to Food Campaign have been doing for years. The road will undoubtedly be long and difficult, but it is worth remembering that, despite the suffering that still exists in the world, there also have been profound victories. Consider that a global commitment to universalising basic child health measures – especially immunisation, breastfeeding promotion, and oral rehydration salts for diarrhoeal treatment – has saved the lives of over 20 million children over the past three decades. Consider that ten years ago, being HIV-positive in a poor country was an automatic death sentence; now, thanks chiefly to peoples' movements all over the world, millions of HIV-positive people have affordable access to treatment that will extend their life by decades, and the hope that *every* HIV-infected man, woman and child in the world will be able to access treatment in the near future has gone from being scorned as naïve idealism to being regarded as a realistic possibility. Consider also that, in rich countries, benefits for the elderly and disabled are considered to be no less than rights that the government has a legal obligation to provide, not charity or 'discretionary' assistance; as the International Labour Organisation often notes, these types of rights-based social protection measures for the vulnerable have been among humanity's finest achievements of the past century.

The list could go on, but the point is this: the end of hunger may seem impossibly idealistic now, but the work of people will ensure that 'impossible' will one day no longer be so. Hunger is preventable; it must be prevented. Let us begin the work, together.

Figure 4.1   Soybean field of the Umodze project, Kasiya, Malawi.

Copyright © S. Hauenstein Swan.

Appendix: The Cost of a Minimum Essential Intervention Package to Fight Seasonal Hunger

COMMUNITY-BASED MANAGEMENT OF ACUTE MALNUTRITION

Estimated Global Cost: £0.96–£1.87 billion

Community-based management (CBM) approaches have only begun to be piloted on a large scale in the past several years. At this stage, precise costs for a global scale-up of CBM are difficult to determine, but some rough estimates are possible. Of the 55 million acutely malnourished children in the world under age five, around 19 million are estimated by the World Health Organisation to be severely malnourished.[1] It is this latter group that is the key target for therapeutic feeding. The per-child cost of CBM will vary by local context. The two primary variables are: 1) the potential for RUFs to be manufactured locally, which would reduce the cost of imports; and 2) the quality of the existing health infrastructure for case-finding, delivery of RUFs, follow-up household visits, and so on. Collins et al. (2006) report costs per admission at two established emergency CBM programmes at between £50 and £99, although this seems to be declining in recent years as CBM approaches are standardised and made more efficient. Using this range as an estimate, however, amounts to between £0.96 and £1.87 billion for 19 million children, including the costs of RUF production.

Of the 19 million acutely malnourished children in the world, between 70 per cent and 90 per cent do not have complications that require inpatient care, and can be treated using CBM protocols only. By emphasising community mobilisation and active case-finding, most recent CBM programmes have come closer to the higher end of this range.[2] If we use the 80 per cent estimate given in the UN joint statement on CBM,[3] about 3.8 million children will require inpatient care. The costs of inpatient care to the implementing agency varies depending on the type and duration of treatment required by the individual child, the quality of existing health care infrastructure and other factors, but they seem to generally fall in a similar range as CBM approaches[4] (the costs to the household, however, may be significantly greater for inpatient care, due to travel costs and absence from work or domestic obligations). Thus, within the £0.96 to £1.87 billion cost estimate given above, between £190 and £375 million would go towards treating children in inpatient facilities. If inpatient therapeutic feeding coverage is to be expanded quickly for all children who require it, temporary therapeutic feeding centres may have to be constructed. Ideally, however, inpatient nutritional treatment units would be available in permanent facilities, such as primary health care clinics, hospitals and other health facilities. The costs of setting up such units in the existing health care system will add greatly to the estimates above.

The figures pertain only to the use of RUFs for severely acutely malnourished children. However, RUFs may have value for treating the more than 40 million moderately acutely malnourished preschool children in the world as well. In 2006, the large-scale use of RUFs in supplementary feeding programmes for moderately malnourished children under age three in the Maradi region of Niger reduced the seasonal spike in severe acute malnutrition significantly. Weight gain among the treated children was considerably higher than that typically seen among moderately malnourished children given the standard supplementary food ration of blended flour.[5] As strong protocols for use of RUFs in supplementary feeding of moderately malnourished children are not yet developed, cost estimates are difficult at this stage, but will likely at least double the £0.96–1.87 billion figure quoted above for treatment of severely acutely malnourished children.

EMPLOYMENT GUARANTEE SCHEMES

Estimated Global Cost: £15–£27 billion

In Chapter 3, we discussed the potential of India's National Rural Employment Guarantee Scheme (NREGS). While the implementation of NREGS remains imperfect, the potential of the programme marks a watershed in the history of rights-based anti-hunger approaches; and the courage and tenacity shown by the country's right to food movement may yet preserve the promise of NREGS.

The price tag of an NREGS-type policy in all countries will not be cheap, but as the legal right to work on demand is the best fundamental defence against seasonal hunger, the results will be worth the cost. Although minimum wages differ from country to country, let us assume an average minimum wage of £1/day, ideally indexed to the price of a given food basket in countries that do not have a food price stabilisation policy. Following the lines of India's programme, 100 days of employment could be offered every year to each household, for an overall transfer of £100/year/household. The commonly accepted estimate is that about 850 million people in the world are undernourished,[6] equalling roughly 200 million households. Let us then assume that between 50 per cent and 90 per cent of these households take up the opportunity of employment (thus far in India, a little over 50 per cent of rural households have enrolled, but only around 12 per cent have actually been provided employment; both these percentages will most likely increase greatly in the coming years). The wage costs would then be between £10 and £18 billion. In India, the wage costs have averaged about two-thirds of the total programme costs, although this total varies from state to state.[7] Assuming the same for our calculations, the total programme costs increase to between £15 and £27 billion.

This is admittedly an indicative calculation, as poverty lines, administrative expense, total enrolment and other factors will vary greatly between countries. But the estimate gives a rough sense of the resources required to provide employment to all those who are vulnerable to seasonal hunger and able to work.

SOCIAL PENSIONS

Estimated Global Cost: £6.03–£12.21 billion

As we discussed in Chapter 2, employment programmes will not meet the needs of those unable to work, especially the elderly. Although these groups are exposed to hunger year-round, rising prices during the lean season deepens their vulnerability. Social pensions will be needed to assist these groups.

Many countries already do have some form of pension scheme for the elderly; in this costing exercise, we concentrate on the poorest countries only, where over 30 million people above the age of 65 currently live, a number that is projected to increase to 60.8 million by the year 2050.[8] The value of the pension varies greatly among the countries that have existing social pension systems, but here we suggest that the 50p/day international extreme poverty line is a good benchmark. This is around 27 per cent of the per-capita income of the 'least developed' country group as a whole, which is around the percentage the most generous existing social pension systems in Africa and Asia currently provide.[9]

A 50p/day social pension to each of the approximately 30 million elderly currently living in the poorest countries would amount to £5.48 billion. This would increase to £11.1 billion by the year 2050. Administrative costs for universal social pensions are generally quite low; increasing the above figures by 10 per cent to account for administrative costs would yield estimates of £6.03 and £12.21 billion.

COMMUNITY-BASED GROWTH PROMOTION

Estimated Global Cost: £3.82–£7.44 billion

The value of integrated child growth promotion services for addressing seasonal hunger is clear. Growth monitoring systems can identify seasonal weight loss in its early stages, before a child becomes severely malnourished, and thus provide a trigger for preventative treatment. Knowledge and nutritional support to pregnant and lactating women increases the likelihood that children, as well as mothers, will suffer less nutritional damage during the hunger season. Supplementary feeding guarantees a minimum amount of food year-round.

The major expenses for a child growth promotion programme relate to wages for personnel and the cost of supplementary food. While annual per-child costs for the variety of growth promotion programmes around the world vary widely,[10] the UN and others have estimated that effective programmes *without* supplementary feeding components generally fall within the £2.50–£5 per person per year range. A smaller investment risks having little or no impact at all.[11] The addition of supplementary feeding doubles this cost; with targeted supplementary feeding for the most vulnerable, costs fall in the £5.50–£9 per person per year range.[12] Assuming universal coverage of the approximately 600 million children under five years old living in poor countries, this latter range would amount to between £3.3 and £5.4 billion in annual costs. This is a considerable expense, but one that should be seen as absolutely necessary to fight malnutrition in the long term.

Adding micronutrient provision to growth promotion programmes would be expensive, but valuable – seasonality affects diet diversity as much as diet quantity, as we saw in the case of Devison Banda's family and the people of Annapanenivari Gudem and Jaklair in India. The two most important micronutrients to consider in a supplementation programme are vitamin A and iron.[13] The cost of providing vitamin A to preschool children in twice-a-year mega-doses falls in the range of 50p–£1.28 per child.[14] At an approximate global population of 600 million preschool children, this equals between £300 and £768 million for universal coverage. The lion's share of the cost comes not in the price of the capsules themselves, but in the 75 per cent of expenses that goes to transport and delivery.[15] Iron supplementation, meanwhile, requires daily or weekly doses to be provided. The target group is also larger: besides young children, it is essential to cover pregnant women, lactating mothers and adolescent girls, all groups highly vulnerable to anaemia. The World Bank (2006) estimates an annual per-participant cost of 28p–£1.59, which would equal between £220 million to £1.27 billion for all groups.

The total estimated cost of universalising growth promotion programmes containing vitamin A and iron supplementation components would be between £3.82 and £7.44 billion.

Notes

PREFACE

1. Lacey (2008). The 'perfect storm' quotation, taken from the article, comes from President Elías Antonio Saca of El Salvador.
2. UN Millennium Project Task Force on Hunger (2005).
3. Lack of reliable agro-climatic, food consumption and nutritional data makes exact estimates of the number affected by seasonal hunger difficult. Ferro-Luzzi and Branca (1993) estimate a global figure of at least 300 million people who 'should be considered at risk for functional and metabolic impairment following their exposure to seasonal bottlenecks in energy turnover that exceed the body's physiological tolerance' (p. 162). However, their analysis is limited to: a) adults only; b) primary malnutrition caused by insufficient food intake, and not secondary malnutrition caused by seasonal disease which limits nutrient absorption and retention; and c) a limited set of countries – 19 in Sahelian Africa, plus India and China. Expanding the analysis to cover children, malnutrition caused by disease, and a larger set of countries, would likely expand the 300 million number considerably. In any case, those affected by seasonal hunger comprise the majority, probably the vast majority, of the 600 million rural people in the world thought to be hungry. In addition, the remainder – those who suffer from a year-round 'chronic' hunger – are not immune to seasonal cycles. Insofar as they are dependent on the agricultural economy, their hunger will also deepen in the pre-harvest months.

1 THOSE WITH COLD HANDS

1. FAO (1989).
2. Personal communication, Jamie Anderson, International Fund for Agricultural Development, Rome.

3. Private moneylenders are often portrayed as the 'bad guys' in the cycle of borrowing and debt that is so common in the rural developing world. There is much truth to the fact that, in the absence of government regulation or competition, a few active lenders can artificially inflate interest rates, just as traders in an uncompetitive market can inflate prices. But moneylenders must also deal with very high default rates, and also lack the means to enforce contracts. Just like traders, they run a risky business, and set interest rates at very high levels partly to cover this risk.

4. Food security experts call the various ways by which families try to ease hunger 'coping strategies' – perhaps a misleading term, since the actions taken come at great cost (as detailed in this section) and thus reflect a *failure* to cope effectively. However, we use the term here to follow convention.

5. Devereux and Tiba (2007).

6. Chambers et al. (1981).

7. Mason et al. (2003).

8. Persson (2005).

9. World Bank (2006).

10. In discussing the links between seasonal hunger and famine in this section, we refer to famines which have crop failure and/or market shocks as their primary cause; but we do not wish to downplay the importance of those famines that are instead caused by conflict or acute natural disaster and thus may not be strongly linked to seasonal hunger.

11. Devereux and Tiba (2007).

12. *Ibid.*

13. Mandala (2005), p. 13.

2   A WORLD FULL OF GOOD IDEAS

1. Chambers et al. (1981), Mandala (2005).

2. Alamgir (1980).

3. Diamond (1997). The factor of geographical luck is detailed in Jared Diamond's narrative of the development of human societies in *Guns, Germs, and Steel*. The simplified version is this: the

greater availability of easily domesticable large-seeded cereal species and easily domesticable animal species in the Fertile Crescent area, as compared to other regions of the world, allowed early development of agriculture there. As these first settled societies began to produce food surpluses, population growth increased and specialisation of labour began – the first classes of ruler-administrators, technological innovators (scientists), and soldiers. The spread of technology and goods was facilitated across Eurasia by the relative lack of geographical barriers along the east–west axis, and over time most of the landmass became technologically far more advanced than the rest of the world. By contrast, civilisations in Africa and the Americas faced formidable climatic and ecological barriers to the diffusion of ideas and technologies along the north–south axis; changes in latitude are harder to adapt to than those of longitude. The Fertile Crescent civilisations eventually collapsed with the degradation of their soils and the subsequent decline of agriculture, and European countries became the pre-eminent powers. By 1492, the 'head-start' in technology – as well as the early exposure to livestock, which immunised Eurasians to many of the diseases that would later decimate New World peoples – had already determined who were to be the winners in the upcoming wars of conquest.

4. Crossgrove et al. (1990), Alamgir (1980), Davis (2001).

5. Sen (1981), Drèze and Sen (1990).

6. Quoted in De Waal (1997), p. 14.

7. Amartya Sen once made the observation that 3 million children die of hunger and hunger-related diseases in India every year, equivalent to the number of deaths that occurred during the Great Bengal Famine in 1943; and yet this annual 'hidden famine' gets very little media and policy attention.

8. Devereux (1992).

9. Ercilla and Chikoko (2006).

10. Mattinen and Ogden (2006).

11. See Barrett and Maxwell (2005) for an extensive overview of the food versus cash debate.

12. WHO et al. (2007).

13. *Ibid.*

14. Médecins Sans Frontières (2007).
15. Collins et al. (2005), Collins et al. (2006), Sadler (2006).
16. Various chapters in Von Braun (1995).
17. Right to Food Campaign (2007).
18. One farmer in discussions during the 1992 drought in Namibia, explaining why everybody in the village helped each other to survive, including through the sharing of pensions, remarked: 'We are all one family here.' To which a neighbour retorted: 'Yes, but your family can eat you!' (Næraa et al. 1993). This is a colourful illustration of the point that social pensions, as with all interventions discussed in this chapter, are inadequate in isolation; their benefits will likely be diluted and their objectives – in the case of pensions, to guarantee that elderly people will have sufficient cash to satisfy their food and other needs – compromised.
19. However, it should not be assumed that people with disabilities need to be automatically excluded from employment programmes, which indeed seems to be a common premise. Employment programmes should make an effort to provide jobs in which people with disabilities can use their particular skills; there have been some attempts to do this under NREGS in India.
20. IIPS and Macro International (2007).
21. Behrman et al. (2004).
22. *Ibid.*
23. Most important among the success factors are: commitment to nutrition at all political levels; participatory planning with the community; the involvement of charismatic community leaders; strong investment into management; health/nutrition awareness trainings; the setting of time-bound objectives; and the involvement of local NGOs.
24. Hunt (2005), Mason et al. (2006).
25. Alderman and Haque (2007).
26. See Gatak and Roy (2007) and Deininger et al. (2007) for recent views on land reform and agricultural productivity in India. See Griffin et al. (2002) and Sender and Johnston (2004) for an overview of opposing positions on the debate. IFAD (2001), chapter 3, lists numerous articles on the topic from countries around the world.

27. Lahiff (2007).

28. World Bank (2007).

29. IFAD (2001).

30. Haile (1988), Wolde-Georgis (2001).

31. Although the graph depicts rainfall for just one village, similar data from other villages across the central Ethiopian highlands confirms both high variability and overall downtrend patterns.

32. Næraa et al. (1993).

33. Devereux and Edwards (2004).

34. IFAD (2001).

35. Devereux (2007c).

36. Dorward et al. (2007), World Bank (2008).

37. Devereux (1999).

38. Kates and Millman (1990).

3   FROM POLICY TO RIGHTS

1. Government of India (2008).

2. Sainath (2007); data from Ministry of Home Affairs, Government of India, as indicated in the article.

3. This is a dated estimate, coming as it does from Ferro-Luzzi and Branca (1993), but chronic energy deficiency estimates from the recent National Family and Health Survey-3 (IIPS and Macro International, 2007) suggest that this number is similar to the present situation.

4. IIPS and Macro International (2007).

5. Rural Development Institute (2007).

6. Monthly income percentages are based on a participatory seasonal calendar exercise we conducted with a group of seven female household heads in Annapanenivari Gudem during March 2008. These households were among the poorest families in the village.

7. *Dhal* is a boiled or fried lentil dish.

8. Hindu Business Line Bureau (2008).

9. Devereux (2000), from other sources listed in Annex 1 of that paper.

10. Sen (1981).

11. Zhou and Wan (2006).
12. Singh (2006).
13. Patnaik (2005).
14. Government of India (2005).
15. The purchased produce is then sold at subsidised prices through the PDS; the difference between the minimum support price outlay and the PDS revenue is the £3 billion cost to the PDS in 2004/05 to which we referred earlier.
16. Centre for Science and Environment (2007).
17. West Godavari District Department of Rural Development (2007).
18. Zeigler (2005).
19. See Right to Food Campaign website at www.righttofoodindia. org for documents pertaining to the original lawsuit and ongoing litigation. The 'founding statement' is also referenced from this website.
20. Right to Food Campaign (2005).
21. See Kent (2005), pp. 147–50, for a proposal of how legal ICDS entitlement can be related to nutritional status, using the example of Tamil Nadu's TINP-II programme.
22. Within the ICESCR, Articles 1 ('In no case may a people be deprived of its own means of subsistence') and 11 ('the right of everyone to an adequate standard of living ... including adequate food'; 'the fundamental right of everyone to be free from hunger') are especially relevant. Articles 24 ('[States parties are bound to] take appropriate measures to combat disease and malnutrition') and 27 ('the right of every child to a standard of living adequate for the child's physical development') in the CRC address child malnutrition and hunger specifically.
23. The United States and Somalia are the only two countries in the world that have not yet ratified the Convention on the Rights of the Child. Nearly 50 countries have not ratified the ICESCR, including the United States.
24. Taken from Zeigler (2002), p. 3.
25. An aside here on the role of social protection in right to food law; the obligation of states vis-à-vis the right to food is usually conceptualised as having three elements – respect, protection, and

fulfilment. To 'respect' implies that the state does not interfere with citizens' means of accessing food (e.g. through land evictions). To 'protect' requires states to ensure that non-state actors do not violate citizens' means of accessing food (e.g. through theft). To 'fulfil' means to actively provide services that enhance access to food. It is within this last category that social protection falls, and it is on this category that we concentrate in this chapter when discussing the right to food, as we believe the obligation to 'fulfil' is of the utmost importance in fighting seasonal hunger and malnutrition. Despite our bias, right to food law needs also to concern itself strongly with the 'respect' and 'protect' categories – particularly (but not exclusively) in times of conflict and other major economic or political shocks.

26. FAO (2005).

27. We wish to emphasise that the list of interventions in the 'minimum essential package' is not an argument that seasonal hunger can be ended by one-size-fits-all blueprint approaches, but rather is an attempt to identify a strong common foundation for food security policy. Part of the difficulty in creating a comprehensive policy agenda to fight seasonal hunger is that the achievement of food security is not seen as a straightforward exercise in 'service delivery' (as contrasted to, for example, perceptions of health care). Rather, the end of hunger is perceived to be entangled in issues of international trade, economic growth and other processes that go far beyond service delivery. There is certainly wisdom in acknowledging the complexity of fighting hunger. But as we have discussed in this book, a basic set of emergency, social protection and agricultural development interventions can take us a long way towards reducing seasonal hunger and malnutrition. Universalising such proven interventions is a good start to creating an institutionalised service delivery-like structure for food security. Similar to the case of health care, implementing these interventions will, of course, always entail more than simple service delivery: it will also require adaptation to cultural, social and economic barriers (for example, constraints associated with gender inequity or the transport and time costs of accessing social protection services). But, much as the major successes in global

public health in the past two decades – for example, promotion of breastfeeding, immunisation, use of oral rehydration salts – have depended on simple, replicable delivery models, basing the foundation of anti-hunger strategies on the same principles will increase the likelihood of rapid impact.

28. Further cost savings can come about by designing creative synergies at the community level between the various components of the minimum package above. For example, employment guarantee programmes can be used to stimulate local RUF production, both in the agricultural production of ingredients and the actual manufacture of RUFs from these ingredients; the RUFs can in turn be used in CBM programmes and in the supplementary feeding component of community-based growth promotion.

29. Zeigler (2002).

30. Kent (2005).

31. Abi-Saab (1994, pp. 29–49), as quoted in Zeigler (2002).

32. As quoted by Von Braun (1995), p. xvi.

4 POSTSCRIPT: ONENESS

1. Chambers et al. (1981).

APPENDIX

1. WHO (2007).

2. Collins et al. (2005) estimate that, in a well designed programme emphasising community mobilisation and active case-finding, 85–90 per cent of severely malnourished children can be treated without inpatient facilities. Collins et al. (2006) state that 74 per cent of children in 21 CBM programmes in Malawi, Ethiopia and Sudan were treated as outpatients, although this number is higher in the more recent CBM programmes than in the earlier attempts. Tectonidis (2006) reports that MSF's large 2005 Niger programme treated 70 per cent of children solely as outpatients. The UN joint statement on Community-Based Management of

Severe Acute Malnutrition (WHO/WFP/UN SCN/UNICEF, 2006) estimates that, if found through active case-finding, 80 per cent of children can be treated at home.

3. WHO/WFP/UN SCN/UNICEF (2006).

4. Collins et al. (2005), Khara and Collins (2004), Collins (2004).

5. MSF (2007).

6. FAO (2006).

7. Drèze and Oldiges (2007).

8. Willmore (2006).

9. *Ibid.*

10. Mason et al. (2003).

11. Hunt (2005).

12. World Bank (2006).

13. Iodine deficiency is the third critical micronutrient-related problem that needs to be addressed. However, a highly successful partnership between UN agencies and the private sector is steadily increasing household access to iodised salt, which is the most effective way to deliver iodine, and so we exclude iodine from the costing calculations in this section.

14. World Bank (2006), calculated from various other sources listed on p. 28 of that document.

15. Hunt (2005).

References and Further Reading

Abi-Saab, G. (1994). 'Les sources du droit international: essai de déconstruction' in M. Rama-Montaldo, *Liber Amicorum en hommage au Professeur Eduardo Jimenez de Aréchaga*. Montevideo, Fundación de Cultura Universitaria.

Alamgir, M. (1980). *Famine in South Asia*. Boston, Oelgeschlager, Gunn and Hain.

Alderman, H. and T. Haque (2007). 'Insurance against covariate shocks: the role of index-based insurance in social protection in low-income countries of Africa'. *World Bank Working Paper 95*. Washington DC, World Bank.

Barrett, C. and D. Maxwell (2005). *Food Aid after Fifty Years: recasting its role*. Routledge, London.

Behrman, J.R., H. Alderman and J. Hoddinott (2004). *Copenhagen Consensus: challenges and opportunities – hunger and malnutrition*. Accessed online 15 May 2008 from www.copenhagenconsensus. com.

Centre for Science and Environment (2007). 'Special: India's rainfed areas'. Accessed 15 May 2008 from www.cseindia.org/programme/nrml/rainfed_specials.htm.

Chambers, R. (1997). *Whose Reality Counts?: putting the first last*. London, Intermediate Technology.

Chambers, R. (2004). *Ideas for Development: reflecting forwards*. Brighton, Institute of Development Studies.

Chambers, R., R. Longhurst and A. Pacey (1981). *Seasonal Dimensions to Rural Poverty*. London, Pinter; Totowa, NJ, Allanheld Osmun.

Cohen, M.N. (1990). 'Prehistoric patterns of hunger'. *Hunger in History: food shortage, poverty, and deprivation*, L.F. Newman and W. Crossgrove, eds. Cambridge, Mass., Blackwell.

Collins, S. (2004). 'Community-based therapeutic care – a new paradigm for selective feeding in nutritional crisis'. *Humanitarian Policy Network Paper 48*. London, Overseas Development Institute.

Collins, S., K. Sadler, N. Dent, T. Khara, S. Guerrero, M. Myatt, M. Saboya and A. Walsh (2005). 'Key issues in the success of community-based management of severe malnutrition'. *Food and Nutrition Bulletin* 27(3): S49–82.

Collins, S., N. Dent, P. Binns, P. Bahwere, K. Sadler and A. Hallam (2006). 'Management of severe acute malnutrition in children'. *Lancet* 368: 1992–2000.

Conroy, A.C. (2006). *Poverty, AIDS, and Hunger: breaking the poverty trap in Malawi*. Basingstoke and New York, Palgrave Macmillan.

Crossgrove, W., D. Egilman and P. Heywood (1990). 'Colonialism, international trade, and the nation-state'. *Hunger in History: food shortage, poverty, and deprivation*, L.F. Newman and W. Crossgrove, eds. Cambridge, Mass., Blackwell.

Davis, M. (2001). *Late Victorian Holocausts: El Niño famines and the making of the Third World*. New York, Verso.

Deininger, K, S. Jin and H. Nagarajan (2007). 'Land reforms, poverty reduction, and economic growth: evidence from India'. *World Bank Policy Research Working Paper* 4448. Washington DC, World Bank.

Devereux, S. (1992). *Household Responses to Food Insecurity in Northeastern Ghana*. DPhil thesis, Oxford University.

Devereux, S. (1999). '"Making Less Last Longer": Informal safety nets in Malawi'. *IDS Discussion Paper* 373. Brighton, Institute of Development Studies.

Devereux, S. (2000). 'Famine in the 20th century'. *IDS Working Paper* 105. Accessed 15 May 2008 from www.ids.ac.uk/ids/bookshop/wp/wp105.pdf.

Devereux, S. (2007a). *The New Famines: why famines persist in an era of globalization*. London and New York, Routledge.

Devereux, S. (2007b). 'What is Social Protection and how does it fit into UNICEF's mandate?' Presentation given at Institute of Development Studies, Brighton, UK.

Devereux, S. (2007c). 'Seasonality and Social Protection in Africa'. Conference paper: *Rural Development: retrospect and prospect*. University of Oxford.

Devereux, S. (2008). 'Targeting social safety nets to support agricultural growth'. Conference paper: *Convergence between Social Service*

Provision and Productivity Enhancing Investments in Development Strategies. Pietermaritzburg, South Africa.

Devereux, S. and J. Edwards (2004). 'Climate change and food security'. *IDS Bulletin* 35(3): 22–30.

Devereux, S. and R. Sabates-Wheeler (2004). 'Transformative social protection'. *IDS Working Paper* 232. Brighton, Institute of Development Studies.

Devereux, S. and Z. Tiba (2007). 'Malawi's first famine, 2001–2002'. *The New Famines: why famines persist in an era of globalization*, S. Devereux, ed. London and New York, Routledge.

De Waal, A. (1997). *Famine Crimes: politics and the disaster relief industry in Africa*. Oxford, James Currey.

Diamond, J. (1997). *Guns, Germs, and Steel: the fates of human societies*. New York, W.W. Norton.

Dorward, A., E. Chirwa, D. Boughton and V. Kelly (2007). 'Evaluation of the 2006/7 Agricultural Input Supply Programme, Malawi'. *Interim Report*. London, Imperial College.

Drèze, J. and C. Oldiges (2007). *How is NREGA doing?* Accessed 15 May 2008 from www.righttofoodindia.com.

Drèze, J. and A.K. Sen (1990). *The Political Economy of Hunger*. Oxford and New York, Clarendon Press and Oxford University Press.

Drèze, J. and A.K. Sen (1992). *Hunger and Public Action*. Oxford and New York, Clarendon Press and Oxford University Press.

Edkins, J. (2002). *Whose Hunger?: concepts of famine, practices of aid*. Minneapolis, University of Minnesota Press.

Ercilla, M.B. and M.P. Chikoko (2006). *Methodology: nutrition and food security surveillance system*. Lilongwe, Action Against Hunger.

Ferro-Luzzi, A. and F. Branca (1993). 'Nutritional seasonality: the dimensions of the problem'. *Seasonality and Human Ecology*, S. Ulijaszek and S. Strickland, eds. Cambridge, Cambridge University Press.

Ferro-Luzzi, A. and International Food Policy Research Institute (IFPRI) (2001). *Seasonal Undernutrition in Rural Ethiopia: magnitude, correlates, and functional significance*. Washington, DC and Rome, International Food Policy Research Institute; Instituto Nazionale della

Nutrizione in collaboration with Ethiopian Health and Nutrition Research Institute, Addis Ababa.

Food and Agriculture Organisation of the United Nations (FAO) (1989). *Prevention of Post-Harvest Food Losses: fruits, vegetables, and root crops: a training manual.* Rome, FAO.

Food and Agriculture Organisation of the United Nations (FAO) (2005). *Voluntary Guidelines to Support the Progressive Realization of the Right to Adequate Food in the Context of National Food Security.* Rome, FAO.

Food and Agriculture Organisation of the United Nations (FAO) (2006). *State of Food Insecurity in the World 2006.* Rome, FAO.

Food and Agriculture Organisation of the United Nations (FAO) (2008a). *FAOSTAT database.* Accessed 29 February 2008 from http://faostat.fao.org.

Food and Agriculture Organisation of the United Nations (FAO) (2008b). *Growing Demand on Agriculture and Rising Prices of Commodities.* Prepared for the Round Table organised for the 31st Session of IFAD's Governing Council, 14 February 2008, by the Trade and Markets and Agricultural Development Economics Divisions. Access 15 May 2008 from www.fao.org/es/esc/common/ecg/538/en/RisingPricesIFAD.pdf.

Gatak, M. and S. Roy (2007). 'Land reform and agricultural productivity in India: a review of the evidence'. *Oxford Review of Economic Policy* 23(2): 251–69.

Gill, G.J. (1991). *Seasonality and Agriculture in the Developing World: a problem of the poor and powerless.* New York and Cambridge, Cambridge University Press.

Government of India (2005). *Performance Evaluation of Targeted Public Distribution System.* Programme Evaluation Organisation, Planning Commission. New Delhi, Government of India.

Government of India (2008). *Union Budget and Economic Survey.* Accessed 18 May 2008 from http://indiabudget.nic.in/ub2008-09/ubmain.htm.

Government of Malawi (2001). *Market Information System: monthly retail market prices.* Lilongwe, Ministry of Agriculture and Irrigation.

Government of Niger / World Food Programme / Food and Agriculture Organisation / United Nations Children's Fund / Famine Early Warning Systems Network (2008). 'Enquête sur la vulnérabilité à l'insécurité alimentaire des ménages', Fevrier 2008.

Gragnolati, M., M. Shekar, M. Das Gupta, C. Bredenkamp and Y. Lee (2005). 'India's undernourished children: a call for reform and action'. *World Bank Health, Nutrition and Population Discussion Paper*. Washington, DC, World Bank.

Griffin, K., A.R. Khan and A. Ickowitz (2002). 'Poverty and the Distribution of Land'. *Journal of Agrarian Change* 2(3): 279–330.

Haile, T. (1988). 'Causes and characters of drought in Ethiopia'. *Ethiopian Journal of Agricultural Sciences* 10(1–2): 85–97.

Hindu Business Line Bureau (2008). 'AP launching Rs/2 kg rice scheme today'. *The Hindu Business Line* 9 April 2008. Accessed 15 May 2008 from www.thehindubusinessline.com/2008/04/09/stories/2008040952352100.htm.

Hunt, J. (2005). 'The potential impact of reducing global malnutrition on poverty reduction and economic development'. *Asia Pacific Journal of Clinical Nutrition* 14 (CD Supplement): 10–38.

International Fund for Agricultural Development (IFAD) (2001). *Rural Poverty Report 2001: the challenge of ending rural poverty*. New York, Oxford University Press.

International Institute for Population Sciences (IIPS) and Macro International (2007). *National Family Health Survey (NFHS-3), 2005–06: India: Volume I*. Mumbai, IIPS.

Kates, R.W. and S. Millman (1990). 'On ending hunger: the lessons from history'. *Hunger in History: food shortage, poverty, and deprivation*, L.F. Newman and W. Crossgrove, eds. Cambridge, Mass., Blackwell.

Kennedy, P.M. (2006). *The Parliament of Man: the past, present, and future of the United Nations*. New York, Random House.

Kent, G. (2005). *Freedom from Want: the human right to adequate food*. Washington, DC, Georgetown University Press.

Khara, T. and S. Collins (2004). 'Community-therapeutic care'. *Emergency Nutrition Network* special supplement 2: 1–55.

Lacey, M. (2008). 'Across globe, empty bellies bring rising anger'. *New York Times* 18 May 2008, online edition.

Lahiff, E. (2007). '"Willing buyer, willing seller": South Africa's failed experiment in market-led agrarian reform'. *Third World Quarterly* 28(8): 1577–97.

Mandala, E.C. (2005). *The End of Chidyerano: a history of food and everyday life in Malawi, 1860–2004.* Portsmouth, NH, Heinemann.

Mason, J., P. Musgrove and J.P. Habicht (2003). 'At least one-third of poor countries' disease burden is due to malnutrition'. *Disease Control Priorities Project Working Paper.* Bethesda, MD, United States National Institutes of Health, Fogarty International Center, Disease Control Priorities Project. No. 1: 40.

Mason, J., R. Soekirman-Galloway, J. Martines, P. Musgrove and D. Sanders (2006). 'Community Health and Nutrition Programmes'. *Disease Control Priorities in Developing Countries.* D. Jamison, J.G. Breman, A.R. Measham, G. Alleyne, M. Claeson, D.B. Evans, P. Jha, A. Mills and P. Musgrove, eds. Washington, DC, World Bank.

Mattinen, H. and K. Ogden (2006). 'Cash-based interventions: lessons from southern Somalia'. *Disasters* 30(3): 297–315.

Médecins Sans Frontières (MSF) / Doctors Without Borders (2007). *Food is Not Enough.* Accessed 15 May 2008 from www.msf.org/source/advocacy/malnutrition/2007/launch/MSF_Food_Is_Not_Enough.pdf.

Næraa, T., S. Devereux, B. Frayne and P. Harnett (1993). 'Coping with drought in Namibia'. *NISER Research Report* 12. Namibian Institute for Social and Economic Research. Windhoek, University of Namibia.

Neelakanteswara Rao, N. (1997). *Famines and Relief Administration: a case study of coastal Andhra, 1858–1901.* New Delhi, Radha Publications.

Newman, L.F. and W. Crossgrove, eds. (1990). *Hunger in History: food shortage, poverty, and deprivation.* Cambridge, Mass., Blackwell.

Patnaik, U. (2005). *Theorizing Food Security and Poverty in the Era of Economic Reforms.* Second Freedom from Hunger lecture, Centre for Environment & Food Security. Accessed 15 May 2008 from www.mfcindia.org/utsa.pdf.

Persson, L.A. (2005). 'The unfinished child survival revolution'. *Scandinavian Journal of Food and Nutrition* 49(4): 146–50.

Right to Food Campaign (2005). *Supreme Court Orders on the Right to Food: a tool for action*. Accessed online 15 May 2008 from www.righttofoodindia.org/data/scordersprimer.doc.

Right to Food Campaign (2007). *Employment Guarantee Act: a primer*. Delhi, Right to Food Campaign.

Rotberg, R.I., T.K. Rabb, et al. (1985). *Hunger and History: the impact of changing food production and consumption patterns on society*. Cambridge and New York, Cambridge University Press.

Rotberg, R.I. and United Nations University, World Hunger Programme (1983). *Imperialism, Colonialism, and Hunger: east and central Africa*. Lexington, Mass., Lexington Books.

Rural Development Institute (2007). *Our Work in India*. Accessed 15 May 2008 from www.rdiland.org/OURWORK/OurWork_India.html.

Russell, S.A. (2005). *Hunger: an unnatural history*. New York, Basic Books.

Sachs, J. (2005). *The End of Poverty: economic possibilities for our time*. New York, Penguin Press.

Sadler, K. (2006). 'Treating acute malnutrition seriously'. Accessed 15 May 2008 from http://nutrition.tufts.edu/docs/media/Sadler_10_10_07.ppt.

Sahn, D.E. and International Food Policy Research Institute (1989). *Seasonal Variability in Third World Agriculture: the consequences for food security*. Baltimore, Johns Hopkins University Press.

Sainath, P. (2007). 'Farm suicides rising, most intense in 4 states'. *The Hindu* 12 November 2007, online edition. Accessed 18 May 2008 from www.hinduonnet.com/2007/11/12/stories/2007111253911100.htm.

Sen, A.K. (1981). *Poverty and Famines: an essay on entitlement and deprivation*. Oxford, Clarendon Press; New York, Oxford University Press.

Sen, A.K. and J. Drèze (1995). *India: economic development and social opportunity*. Oxford and New Delhi, Oxford University Press.

Sender, J. and D. Johnston (2004). 'Searching for a Weapon of Mass Production in Africa: unconvincing arguments for land reform'. *Journal of Agrarian Change* 4(1–2): 142–64.

Singh, S. (2006). *Food Security-Effectiveness of the Public Distribution System in India*. Master degree thesis, University of Ljubljana.

Accessed 15 May 2008 from www.cek.ef.uni-lj.si/magister/singh11-B-06.pdf.

Stiglitz, J.E. and A. Charlton (2005). *Fair Trade For All: how trade can promote development.* Oxford and New York, Oxford University Press.

Tectonidis, M. (2006). 'Crisis in Niger – Outpatient Care for Severe Acute Malnutrition'. *New England Journal of Medicine* 354(3): 224–7.

Ulijaszek, S. and S. Strickland, eds. (1993). *Seasonality and Human Ecology.* Cambridge, Cambridge University Press.

United Nations Millennium Project Task Force on Hunger (2005). *Halving Hunger: it can be done.* P.A. Sánchez, M.S. Swaminathan, P. Dobie and Nalan Yuksei, lead authors. London and Sterling, VA, Earthscan: xxv, 245.

Vaitla, B. and T. Zerihun (2005). *Food Insecurity and Agricultural Development in the Southern Region of Ethiopia.* Addis Ababa: Action Contre La Faim.

Vaitla, B. and T. Zerihun. (2006). *The Performance and Potential of Food Security Interventions in Eastern SNNPR: a closer look at the Safety Nets and Household Extension Package programmes, case studies in Sidama and Gamo Gofa Zones.* Addis Ababa: Action Contre La Faim.

Vernon, J. (2007). *Hunger: a modern history.* Cambridge, Mass., The Belknap Press of Harvard University Press.

Von Braun, J., ed. (1995). *Employment for Poverty Reduction and Food Security.* Washington, DC, International Food Policy Research Institute.

West Godavari District Department of Rural Development (2007). *Action Plan 2007–08.* (Unpublished government document, available upon request from District.)

Willmore, L. (2006). 'Universal Pensions for Developing Countries'. *World Development* 35(1): 24–51.

Wolde-Georgis, T. (2001). *El Niño and Drought Early Warning in Ethiopia.* Accessed 1 September 2005 from www.brad.ac.uk/research/ijas/ijasno2/Georgis.html.

World Bank (2006). *Repositioning Nutrition as Central to Development.* Washington, DC, World Bank.

World Bank (2007). *India: land policies for growth and poverty reduction*. World Bank Report 38298-IN. Washington, DC, World Bank.

World Bank (2008). *World Development Report 2007: agriculture for development*. Washington, DC, World Bank.

World Health Organisation (WHO) (2006). Report of an informal consultation on the community-based management of severe malnutrition in children. Accessed 10 May 2008 from www.who.int/entity/child_adolescent_health/documents/fnb_v27n3_suppl/en/.

World Health Organisation (WHO) (2007). *World Health Statistics, 2007*. Geneva, World Health Organisation.

World Health Organisation (WHO) / World Food Programme (WFP) / United Nations System Standing Committee on Nutrition (UN SCN) / United Nations Children's Fund (UNICEF). (2007). *Community-Based Management of Severe Acute Malnutrition*. Accessed 15 May 2008 from www.unicef.org/media/files/Community_Based_Management_of_Severe_Acute_Malnutrition.pdf.

Zeigler, J. (2002). *The Right to Food: January 2002 report*. United Nations Economic and Social Council report. Accessed 15 May 2008 from www.righttofood.org/ECN4200354.pdf.

Zeigler, J. (2005). *The Right to Food: mission to India*. United Nations Economic and Social Council report. Accessed 15 May 2008 from www.righttofood.org/India%20PDF.pdf.

Zhou, Z. and G. Wan. (2006). 'The public distribution systems of foodgrains and implications for food security: a comparison of the experiences of India and China'. *United Nations University Research Paper* No. 2006/98. New York, United Nations University.

About the Authors

Stephen Devereux is a Research Fellow and a Director of the Centre for Social Protection at the Institute of Development Studies, University of Sussex. He works on food security, rural livelihoods and social protection in Africa, especially in Ethiopia, Ghana, Malawi and Namibia. His books include *Food Security in Sub-Saharan Africa* (co-edited with Simon Maxwell), *Theories of Famine* and *The New Famines*.

Bapu Vaitla is an advocacy and research officer for ACF. He has previous experience in rural development research and project implementation in India and Ethiopia, concentrating on the intersections of hunger, agriculture and social protection. He is currently working on land rights and malnutrition issues in Andhra Pradesh state, India. He was a co-editor for last year's Hunger Watch report, *The Justice of Eating*.

Samuel Hauenstein Swan has been working for humanitarian organisations since 1994, focusing on health, hunger and rights issues. His work looks specifically at the interaction of humanitarian and development assistance with local structures. His publications include: *Women and Hunger*, *The Justice of Eating* (co-edited), *Local Voices: community perspectives on HIV and hunger*. He heads Hunger Watch, ACF's policy and advocacy department.

Robert Chambers is a Research Associate at the Institute of Development Studies, University of Sussex. His current concerns and interests include professionalism, power, the personal dimension in development, participatory methodologies, agriculture and science, seasonality, and community-led total sanitation. His work on seasonality in the 1980s included a co-edited book, *Seasonal Dimensions to Rural Poverty*.

Index

Compiled by Sue Carlton